The Golden Dawn

A Key to Ritual Magic

The Golden Dawn

A Key to Ritual Magic

Gordon Strong

AXIS MUNDI
BOOKS

Winchester, UK
Washington, USA

First published by Axis Mundi Books, 2014
Axis Mundi Books is an imprint of John Hunt Publishing Ltd., Laurel House, Station Approach,
Alresford, Hants, SO24 9JH, UK
office1@jhpbooks.net
www.johnhuntpublishing.com
www.axismundi-books.com

For distributor details and how to order please visit the 'Ordering' section on our website.

Text copyright: Gordon Strong 2013

ISBN: 978 1 78279 579 7

A CIP catalogue record for this book is available from the British Library.

Design: Lee Nash

Printed and bound by CPI Group (UK) Ltd, Croydon, CR0 4YY

We operate a distinctive and ethical publishing philosophy in all
areas of our business, from our global network of authors to
production and worldwide distribution.

CONTENTS

Magick enables us to receive sensible impressions of worlds other than the physical universe...these worlds have their own laws...

Aleister Crowley

There's no hope
No enlightenment
In the quest for knowledge,
Only pain is certain

Arthur Rimbaud

Learn to know all but keep thyself unknown.

Gnostic Maxim

Acknowledgements

Alan Richardson was unstinting in his help and encouragement, as were Jane Marshall and Victoria Brudal. Paul Dunne, a great student of magic, took time out to offer some excellent insights. My friend of over forty years, Dave Moore, delved into his library to find books on W.B. Yeats.

I'm also extremely grateful to Peregrin Wildoak for reading through the manuscript and detecting a few errors that, if allowed to go uncorrected, would have given me sleepless nights for evermore.

Introduction

The 'Order of The Golden Dawn' could be regarded as the magical experiment that went terribly wrong. If we are to be charitable, we may speak of it as 'a noble failure'; if realistic, it was a dream that was always going to become a nightmare. Magic has a volatile energy and it attracts those whose character contains that element. Magic is also, to paraphrase the Ten Commandments, 'a jealous god'. Divine power is the source of all magic and those who attempt to monopolise this universal force, setting themselves up as a rival to God, do not meet with a kind reception.

The triumph of the Golden Dawn was marred by the very elements that also made it successful. It is apparent that the personalities who held a rank within the organisation, and thus were in a position to shape its progress, had an idiosyncratic vision of how the Order should be. Internal politics eventually destroyed the Order proving, if it really needed to be, that the magical world is never able to completely transcend the material plane. The machinations that lay beneath the daily instruction in magical philosophy are thoroughly investigated in our study. Here, events on both sides of the veil have an equal fascination.

The danger of an absolute conviction becoming a mere tyranny are epitomised in the saga of McGregor Mathers. The most celebrated founder of the Order, his behaviour is uncannily reflected in the rise and fall of the Golden Dawn. Mathers' sincerity regarding his involvement with the practice of magic cannot be questioned. The lengths he was prepared to go in his investigations are quite extraordinary in their dedication and intensity. Unfortunately, Mathers' hold on reality, to any real degree, lessened with the years and a fantastic oblivion eventually claimed him.

The Golden Dawn can be seen as synonymous with the birth

of the Western Magical Tradition. The seeds of the great developments in magic during the twentieth century were sown in the last two decades of the C19th. Significant figures such as Dion Fortune (expelled) and Aleister Crowley (also removed), may have initially gained some knowledge from the Order, although only their general impressions are left to us.

It must be kept in mind when assessing the happenings in the Golden Dawn that it was not just an ordinary fellowship or society but a magical order. Its aims were also different to contemporary organisations – the Theosophical Society and the Freemasons. Because the Order was concerned with the practical aspects of magic, an active supernatural current pervaded.

As a practising magician myself, I know full well that the old adages concerning the use of occult powers still hold true. The question asked of the initiate, 'Why do ye seek?' has only one acceptable response, 'I seek in order to serve.' Therein is contained the essential precept of magic – motive. 'Many are called, but few are chosen' would seem also to be pertinent to the whole esoteric business.

In the twenty-first century, despite unlimited access to occult knowledge, there are still very few individuals worthy of the title 'magician'. To have lived in the 1890s meant it was possible to be part of an organisation that offered real initiation into the esoteric world. The Golden Dawn set out to be an 'occult academy' and this ambition made it a revolutionary organisation. It was also offering instruction to both men and women and this was one aspect that made it different.

As the twentieth century approached, the more repressive aspects of Victorian England were gradually disappearing. Change in the social structure could be detected much earlier. The first woman doctor began practising medicine in 1865; Queen Victoria was made Empress of India in 1876; and the first female Member of Parliament took her seat in the House of Commons in 1879. These were hints that a modern world, and more significantly, one that promoted equality, was emerging in Britain.

Not since the time of the ancient Celts had women enjoyed some equal status with men. In that bygone age they had equal share in any conjugal property and if they wished were permitted to divorce their partner. The fight for equality was on! Although even to this day a total victory has never been gained, the battle cry echoed down the decades of the twentieth century. It was particularly strident in the 1960s when the movement forever known, often pejoratively, as 'Women's Lib' was born.

The social and cultural revolution which began in the 1880s gave rise to the 'independent woman'. This new kind of female acknowledged her own femininity and was proud to display that quality, particularly in the way she dressed and the opinions that she held. These pioneers were to eventually break the restrictive mould that had previously made them 'mirrors of men'. A strong reaction to the Judaeo Christian teachings that many women saw as overly patriarchal, determined the spiritual path that many were to follow.

From the ranks of these 'superwomen' came the individuals who would play such an important part in the Golden Dawn. Women did not dominate the Golden Dawn but their presence was always felt in the Order. They were a countermelody to the more strident themes trumpeted by their male counterparts. The women of the Golden Dawn were able to instil an original approach to magic, one that relied on dedication and discipline combined with a trust in their intuition.

Such a combination of qualities exactly opposed the 'flightiness' attributed to women by those who wished to denigrate them. That the female members of the Golden Dawn were held in high respect by the majority of the Order, rather than simply being tolerated, indicates an enormous sea-change. It seemed as if this radical new energy originated within the Inner Planes – the Goddess exerting her influence.

The essential 'Englishness' of the Golden Dawn is a factor in its development that cannot be ignored. Under this title must go such things as formality, punctiliousness and a love of ceremony. Yet beneath the surface, as always in England, there lay a desire to subvert, to throw over the constraints of convention. A sense of humour, a gentle mocking, was never far away. Behind the mask of conservatism was always the Imp of Misrule.

Our study does not seek to be a feminist tract; it is rather an investigation into whether both men and women were able to practise magic with equal power at a particular time. It seems too obvious to recall that this essential polarity of male and female was the basis of Egyptian and Celtic magic many thousands of years previously. Since that time the notion of priest and priestess performing rituals together had been unseen in the West. Thus the notion of both sexes having an equal role in magical practice must have seemed very radical. The cult of Isis and Osiris, for instance, was probably known only to a very small minority. It is little wonder that Macgregor and Moina Mathers, were eager to revive rites that took the god and goddess as their theme.

Not only did the Golden Dawn embrace 'new women' (during its fifteen years of existence more than one third of the Order would be female) it drew the cream of thinking society. Literature, the stage, radical politics, and art came together in the Order. It is easy to imagine they would have mingled in an atmosphere of mystery and excitement.

The Golden Dawn was more than just a magical club however, it was a nexus of new ideas and perspectives. In this burgeoning of sexual equality, and perhaps yearning for a neat and well-rounded tale, one might have wished that for every priestess there was a corresponding priest. Was this to be? As Dion Fortune remarked,

My two selves have never been permanently in me, for no human physique would stand that; nor can I invoke my higher self at will, but I know how to make the conditions that cause it to come in. Unfortunately that is a thing in which I always need to have help; I cannot do it single-handed; someone has to see the Goddess in me, and then She manifests.[1]

Such a relationship clearly existed in the pairing of Macgregor Mathers and Moina, his wife. It was there with other men and women in the Order, but never quite with the overwhelming intensity that existed between the Mathers. The Golden Dawn teachings may also have enlightened certain individuals in their approach to personal relationships. The Order strove, through its teachings, to provide self-realization for the initiate, and those who joined were pioneers, men and women venturing into a new kind of consciousness. They were determined to discover other worlds of meaning not readily available on the earthly plane.

It is appropriate at this point to briefly mention the theoretical studies that the neophyte was expected to undertake. In these initial stages, a study of astrology and the Tarot would provide insights into how the 'magical persona' could be tempered and improved. Beginners familiarised themselves with the archetypes in the Western Magical Tradition, and the 'magical imagination' was developed with the aid of meditation, and by making talismans and magical weapons.

The history of the Golden Dawn is a tale of passions, intrigues, quarrels and obsessions. Such emotions, combined with magic, produced a powerful elixir. The Golden Dawn was rightly named; it did mark a golden age, but one with a wondrous beginning and an ignominious end. Perhaps those involved, being mere mortals, could not be expected to be able to control and sustain the power that had been bestowed upon them.

I live not far from the city of Bristol where the 'Hermes Lodge' of the Golden Dawn functioned intermittently until 1970. As other lodges fell away and ceased to be, it became the repository of their artefacts. I made an astonishing personal discovery in

2010 when, after giving a talk on Madame Blavatsky at the Bristol Theosophical Society, I was introduced to Lucy Hilliar. To my astonishment, she announced that she possessed certain Golden Dawn artefacts, these had come to her by way of the Hermes Lodge. It seemed that twenty-five years after the closure of the Lodge a collection of artefacts had been put into auction.

Tragically, the bulk of these disappeared, perhaps lost forever. However, I did examine what still existed of the original collection. There were only a few items, but they still had a tremendous resonance. Books once owned, and signed individually, by the two Mathers and Waite, were a delight to handle. Most fascinating were the packs of Tarot Cards, originally blank and subsequently coloured by various members of the Lodge as part of their magical instruction. The designs upon the cards were those executed by Westcott one of the founders of the Golden Dawn, one of the principal figures in our study. Thus, I am able to say that I have experienced at first hand something of the power of The Golden Dawn.

Gordon Strong
Portishead
U.K.

September 2010

I

An Extraordinary Birth

The whole universe, under the stimulation of the magical elements... seems to tumble like a pack of cards crazily about one's feet.
Israel Regardie

To have lived in the closing decades of the nineteenth century is a dream dear to the hearts of many, and not only those involved in the esoteric world. During this late Victorian period, artists and thinkers in the West craved a significant spiritual dimension in their lives. As the nineteenth century had unfurled, dissatisfaction with science and the tenets of the Establishment had increased. As Gurdjieff once suggested, 'The flight to the Secret Traditions represents an escape from insignificance...Man is...capable of divinity...'[2]

For those in the West who wished to pursue a transcendental path, there were a limited number of options available. Freemasonry had attracted followers since the early 1800s; The Ancient and Archaeological Order of Druids was founded in 1874; and Madame Blavatsky's Theosophical Society came to be a year later in 1875. These organisations, although worthy in their own right, would not have provided practical instruction in magic if that was what an individual sought to discover. Hence *The Esoteric Order of The Golden Dawn,* came to fill a significant gap in any study of the occult.

The order was inaugurated in 1888. The organization advertised itself plainly as a 'school of magic'. Its founders – Samuel MacGregor Mathers, William Woodman and William Westcott – promised to reveal all manner of occult knowledge and give practical instruction in the art to initiates. Astral travelling, evoking elemental spirits, scrying, alchemy, rituals of power and majesty – all were included in the curriculum.[3]

For the ordinary Victorian in England, the 1880s was the decade that brought Gilbert and Sullivan's operettas, the adoption of Greenwich Mean Time, and the gruesome murders perpetrated by Jack the Ripper to their lives. In various corners of society other more far-reaching changes began to occur. Some men and women desired to involve themselves in 'spiritual' matters. Their numbers would increase with the years, and the movement would culminate in the 'New Age' movement that had its beginnings in the twentieth century and flourishes greatly today.

At the outset, the Theosophical Society was important to this transcendental shift. Madame Blavatsky's appeal was not confined to an obscure section of society; luminaries such as Einstein and James Joyce were prepared to embrace her principles. Helena Petrovna Blavatsky, with the aid of Colonel William Olcott, inaugurated the Theosophical Society in 1875 in New York. In 1878, Charles Massey founded the London Lodge of the Society. A remarkable woman – Anna Kingsford – succeeded him and became President of the Lodge in 1883. Edward Maitland, her platonic partner, described her as,

Tall, slender, and graceful in form. Fair and exquisite in complexion. Bright and sunny in expression. The hair long and golden, but the brows and lashes dark and the eyes deep set and hazel, and by turns dreamy and penetrating. The mouth rich, full and exquisitely formed.[4]

Kingsford was the author of *The Perfect Way*, a collection of essays on Theosophy, some written before the she actually became part of the Society. These, however, were considered to give her all the right qualifications for a senior position. Unfortunately, many of the Theosophists felt uncomfortable with her role as a Christian mystic. During her tenure Kingsford set about eradicating the influence of the 'Eastern Masters.' As Blavatsky herself was totally dedicated to Kuthumi and El Moyra, it is little wonder that such a radical stance inevitably put a severe strain on the unity of the Lodge. It did not take long before there was a split in the ranks. Blavatsky intervened, and a compromise was reached. The Kingsford set would form a 'Hermetic Lodge' of the Theosophical Society, one that was affiliated but not attached to the main body.

The group's interests were essentially varied – Christian Pantheism, the Qabalah, the mythology of Egypt, and the Tarot. In an intriguing sequel, Blavatsky set up her own Esoteric Group, six months after the Golden Dawn had begun its life. It may be that the Golden Dawn's readiness to admit women came about as a result of Blavatsky and Kingsford. They both had a particularly strong influence upon the two gentlemen who now enter our tale.

Among the speakers to address Kingsford's 'Hermetic Society' were W. Wynn Westcott and S.L. MacGregor Mathers. Both were Masons, Westcott being initiated in 1871 and Mathers in 1877. In his address, Mathers spoke on alchemy and after his talk was apparently very taken by Kingsford. It is said that he eschewed tobacco and became a vegetarian from that moment on, entirely because of conversing with her. As we shall see, this was probably the first and last time Mathers was swayed by another's opinion.

Kingsford was a strident anti-vivisectionist. She knew that Louis Pasteur, the microbiologist and inventor of vaccines, used dogs for his experiments. In a sinister episode, some claim she and a male accomplice planned to murder Pasteur by magical means. Given Mathers probable infatuation with Kingsford, and his own magical skills, could he have been directly involved in such a plot?

Samuel Liddell Mathers had little formal education, leaving school at sixteen. Apart from his Masonic interests, little is known about how he employed himself during the next fifteen years. However, at the age of thirty-one he moved from his home town of Bournemouth to London. In 1882 he can be seen in a studio photograph dressed in the uniform of a lieutenant of the Militia Artillery. This was an assumed rank. He was never commissioned, remaining a private during his entire army career, such as it was. His claim to belong to the Militia Artillery was also false; his regiment was the First Hampshire Infantry Volunteers.

His enthusiasm for military matters is evident in his first published work, *Practical Instruction in Infantry Campaigning Exercises*, a manual for the British Army produced in 1884. Why he continually chose to picture himself as a great warrior chieftain is an interesting question. Was this merely a case of needing to aggrandize himself, or a more serious psychological issue? The intensity and variety of Mathers' delusions, particular of a martial turn, were to increase over the years.

Established in London, after the death of his mother in 1885, Mathers' life began to assume some purpose. After making the acquaintance of Westcott and Woodman, he began to study the occult in earnest. Westcott apparently commissioned Mathers to translate various documents, but no record exists as to what these were. He also met Kenneth Mackenzie, a figure who would soon assume a greater significance in his destiny and also that of Westcott.

A.E. Waite, another significant figure in the shaping of the Golden Dawn, has left us this brief sketch of Mathers at this time.

> ...(he was a) strange person, with rather fish-like eyes...The more I saw of him the more eccentric he proved to be...a combination of Don Quixote and Hudibras, but with a vanity all his own.[5]

In later years, William Wynn Westcott would prove to be almost as enigmatic character as Mathers. At the time of the gestation of the Golden Dawn he seemed to be the *deus ex machine* of the society. His personal vision was to found a school for the 'study of classical medieval occult science'. This profile of him, recorded when the Order was well-established, seems to emphasize his personable manner.

To his students in the Golden Dawn Westcott must have seemed a darling old pussy-cat of man – plump, docile, scholarly, industrious, addicted to regalia and histrionics...if he could avoid saying boo to a goose he would do so...[6]

Every member of the Golden Dawn had their own motto. Westcott chose *Sapere Aude* (Dare to be wise). Considering the outcome of events, and his role in them, these sentiments resonate with a certain irony. In 1912, nearly a decade after the Order's demise he wrote, 'I claim right and precedence in the origin of the G.D.'[7] His view seems to be largely correct, although there was in Westcott's character a marked propensity for fantasy, if not gross fabrication. R.A. Gilbert, one of the foremost researchers of the history of the Golden Dawn, always considered that Westcott 'never was many things that he appeared to be.'[8]

Certainly, Westcott was content to retire into his own world as soon as the Golden Dawn was established. He absolved himself of all real authority and very quickly began to play a secondary role to Mathers. It seems that the particular character of these two men may have contributed to the demise of the Golden Dawn. Gilbert proposes that it was 'destroyed as much by his (Westcott's) timidity as by Mathers' paranoia.'[9] But this is to anticipate.

Westcott was a pillar of Victorian respectability. In the 1890s he held a very responsible position as Coroner for North-East London. His 'other life', was his involvement not only in Freemasonry, but occultism 'beyond the Craft', which indicates that he ventured beyond the usual conventions of the Brotherhood. He joined various other orders, the most significant being the 'Rite of Swedenborg' with which he became affiliated in 1876. Confusingly, this organization had nothing whatever to do with Emmanuel Swedenborg. The Swedish philosopher and mystic's writings included a claim that he could readily visit heaven and hell whenever he wished to do so. The 'Rite' was merely a short-lived venture, the members of which convened in Weston-super-Mare, a 'watering place' in the south-west of England. It was this unlikely location (considering its later notoriety as a holiday resort) that would later host the Osiris Temple of the Golden Dawn.

In 1880, Westcott was introduced to Dr. William Robert Woodford, a man considerably his senior in age. He was a specialist in esoteric studies and Supreme Magus of the Rosicrucian Society. Westcott, almost immediately, joined their ranks. It would be with Woodford that the plans for establishing the Golden Dawn would be drawn up.

Westcott described his new acquaintance as 'an excellent Hebrew scholar, and one of the few English masters of the Hebrew Kabbalah.'[10] Woodman remains a shadowy presence in the history of the Golden Dawn. He had a passion for gardening and was undoubtedly bookish – constantly suggesting pedantic and ponderous volumes for the Order library. No records have survived of any lectures he may have delivered, and only a few scraps of his writing remain.

Much of the Golden Dawn teaching is based upon rites that feature in Rosicrucian and Masonic practice. A link between these two institutions is hotly disputed by Freemasons, yet these lines of poetry from the seventeenth century seem to confirm the notion. Written by Henry Adamson in the *Muses Threnodies*,

For what we do presage is not in grosse
For we brethren of the Rosie Crosse;

We have the Mason Word and second sight
Things for to come we can foretell aright.[11]

In 1866, Robert Wentworth Little founded the *Societa Rosicruciana in Anglia* (Rosicrucian Society of England). He was aided by K.R.H. Mackenzie who became its Supreme Magus after Little. Mackenzie was a man of varying temper, described as companionable when sober but a vicious bully when not so. Reputed to have met Eliphas Levi in Paris in 1861, he was to make a major contribution to the birth of the Golden Dawn.

When Mackenzie died, certain papers were left in the possession of his widow. These documents, which would hereafter be known as the 'Cipher Manuscripts', were acquired by Woodman and later given to Westcott. Once these were in his hands, Westcott saw fit to make very substantial claims for their content. He announced that the manuscripts were explicit instructions from the original German order of the 'Golden Dawn – 'Die Goldene Dammerung'. These, he insisted, contained written permission to inaugurate 'The Hermetic Order of the Golden Dawn' in Britain. It was upon this assertion by Westcott that the entire edifice that is the Order of the Golden Dawn rested. As we shall see, Westcott's insistence that the manuscripts were genuine would later prove to be for him not the Grail, but a poisoned chalice.

A certain Rev. Adolphus F.A. Woodford provided some additional provenance to these manuscripts. An elderly cleric and well-known Masonic author, he owned records which intimated that Eliphas Levi once owned the ciphers. He claimed that these particular papers,

...came...from France with a history that they had passed through Levi's hands and indeed a loose page among them has a note signed A.L.C.[12]

The letters 'A.L.C.' may refer to Alphonse Levi Constantine the baptismal name of Levi, or they may not. Although it is certainly possible that Levi owned the ciphers, it seems highly unlikely. With hindsight it can be seen that Westcott's behaviour is highly suspicious, and that the proof of authenticity he offered was feeble and inadequate.

What are these manuscripts? They consist of graded rituals and the syllabus for a course of instruction in the Qabalah and Hermetic magic: astrology, the tarot, geomancy and alchemy. They are written in a cipher form, one probably created by Mackenzie and others. The method used to construct them is the *Trithemius Cipher*. This is a reasonably simple system of coding invented in the 1850s by Johannes Trithemius, Abbot of the Benedict Monastery of Spanheim. The folios are drawn in black ink and the paper is watermarked 1808.

In some ways conveniently, the main protagonists of this episode – Mackenzie, Hockley and Woodford – all died within the years 1885-1887. Dr. Woodman died in obscurity in 1891. None were ever quizzed further on the matter, so it is impossible to establish any further credence about the said documents.

Westcott's most far-reaching claim was that he discovered among the papers the address of Fraulein Sprengel, a Rosicrucian adept living in Germany. Sprengel was supposedly the existing legatee of *Die Goldene Dammerung* – The Golden Dawn. Westcott claimed that he communicated with Sprengel and subsequently obtained from her permission to found an English branch of the Order. The actual existence of anyone called Anna Sprengel now seems exceedingly doubtful.

Ellic Howe, in his customarily thorough manner, examined six documents – memoranda, letters and messages – pertaining to be written by Fraulein Sprengel, or communications with her. He had 'the invaluable help of Herr Oskar Schlag of Zurich',[13] an eminent graphological and suspect documents specialist. His brief was to ascertain whether these documents were faked. After collating the evidence, it is Howe's conclusion that Fraulein Sprengel was indisputably a mythical figure invented by Westcott.

Later communications by Sprengel are, in Howe's description 'remarkably banal'. This did not matter at the time, for they simply supported Westcott's continuing assertion that she existed. When Sprengel was no longer of any use to Westcott he put it about that she had died. He probably considered he had sewn up the whole business very neatly. Unfortunately for him, the fictitious German lady would, in bizarre circumstances, return to haunt him as we shall see later.

Alternative theories as to the origin of the Cipher Manuscripts have always circulated. Whether these add to their credence, or serve to further condemn them as forgeries, is debatable. Without listing all of these versions, it is useful to examine a trio of them. Arthur Machen, a writer of occult fiction who had joined the Golden Dawn in 1899 promoted the idea that Woodford found the Cipher Manuscript in a second-hand bookstall on Wellington Road in London. In 1923 he wrote,

A gentleman interested in occult studies... was examining a particular volume...he found between the leaves a few pages of dim manuscript...the gentleman bought the book, and when he got home eagerly examined the manuscript...on a separate slip laid next to it – was the address of a person in Germany.[14]

Later Machen, writing in a satirical tone, admitted,

I like the story; but there was not one atom of truth in it. The Twilight Star was a stumer[15]...Its originators must have had some knowledge of Freemasonry; but so ingeniously was this occult fraud put upon the market', that to the best of my belief, the flotation remains a mystery to this day. But what an entertaining mystery; and after all, it did nobody any harm.[16]

It has always been suggested that the rituals were written by Edward Bulwer-Lytton, known for his occult novels *Zanoni* and *A Strange Story*. Another candidate was Frederick Hockley, 'a seer and transcriber of occult manuscripts'. The simplest, and perhaps the most plausible explanation, is that Westcott, Mackenzie, and possibly others, concocted the material themselves. The Golden Dawn syllabus for initiation is not that different from Masonic and Rosicrucian magical theory of the day and would certainly have been familiar to the parties mentioned.

Once he had started, Westcott kept up the pace and did not hesitate to establish further 'credentials' for the Order. In 'The Historic Lecture for Neophytes', he claimed all manner of occult figures were original members of the Golden Dawn. In his lectures he allied the Rosicrucian Order to the Golden Dawn and assured all who expressed an interest in the new Order that it would exactly reproduce the mystic rites of Egypt, Persia and Chaldea. He further claimed that the Golden Dawn was the true inheritance of 'The Secret Wisdom of the Ancient Ages', and thus supreme credence was bestowed upon it. His words must have impressed his listeners as, after his lectures, many sought to immediately join the Order.

Others in the organization had not been idle either. A charter for The Golden Dawn was designed and executed probably by Mather's future wife, Moina Bergson, who was studying at the Slade School of Art at the time. Mathers' own contribution was to produce the first of an impressive collection of elaborate rituals to be used for initiation within the Order.

Opinions differ as to Mathers' scholarship. A.E. Waite described him as a 'comic Blackstone of occult lore' and W.B. Yeats said that he had 'much learning...much imagination, and imperfect taste'. Contrary to this, his ardent supporter, J.W. Brodie-Innes championed Mathers, praising his 'wonderful learning in strange bypaths of knowledge'. Much of the content of the rituals has the true power of a high magician. The words are those of one who believes that divine forces guide his pen. All magicians know the sensation of a ritual writing itself, the scribe merely recording the voices of the gods. Despite his faults, and there were many, the unswerving loyalty of Mathers to the principles of magic can never be questioned.

Other views of the birth of the Order should be mentioned, particularly those of a mystic and most celebrated poet. W.B. Yeats is the most well-known member of the Golden Dawn with Aleister Crowley. Twenty five years after the founding of the Order, he wrote this allegorical account of how it occurred:

> Then an old woman came, leaning upon a stick, and sitting close to them, took up the thought where they had dropped it. Having expounded the whole principle of spiritual alchemy, and bid them found the Order of the Alchemical Rose, she passed from among them, and when they would have followed was nowhere to be seen.[17]

The heady mixture that would eventually rise as the Golden Dawn was now leavening. The ingredients were a combination of occult lore, as much scholarship as could be mustered, and a great many fanciful imaginings. It was from these that the authority of the Golden Dawn as a *bona fide* magical order was created.

On March 1, 1888, the London Temple of the Golden Dawn – *Isis-Urania* – was founded. From the beginning, Westcott appeared to be planning for the inauguration of certain local lodges. He would later establish these in various towns in England. Westcott's first Golden Dawn temple was styled No.3. He explained that Sprengel's Lodge was No.1 and that, rather mysteriously, unnamed others had attempted to inaugurate a No.2 lodge.

The Order promised to offer instruction in magical theory and practice. There was to be a hierarchical system of advancement, and a series of rituals that would eventually guarantee a sublime initiation. Westcott insisted that there be ten grades of initiation to correspond with the ten Sephiroth upon the Qabalistic Tree of Life. This was somewhat spurious as The Supernal Triad – that of *Kether, Chokmah* and *Binah* – were not actually included in the attainable grades.

All this appeared to be much more impressive than anything the Theosophical Society could offer, yet no animosity was apparent between the two organizations. In fact, the June 1889 issue of Blavatsky's Theosophical periodical *Lucifer* included an announcement inviting new members to join the Golden Dawn. Westcott's tactic was to promote an exclusive club, suitable only for those of the 'right sort'. He was shrewd enough to know that the Order had to be different from anything that had gone before. This was to be an organization that reflected a new approach to the spiritual and, more pertinently, the occult. His belief that the Golden Dawn should be a relatively closed organization, unlike the Theosophical Society which was open to all comers, was shrewd. Its exclusive nature was to prove an attraction, rather than a deterrent. Westcott promised new members that,

the Golden Dawn, of which you have now become a member can show you the way to much secret knowledge and spiritual progress...[18]

It is interesting that among those who enrolled in the Golden Dawn during its fifteen years of existence were several figures not usually associated with the occult. They included the writer Algernon Blackwood and Constance Wilde. Certain well-known personalities are sometimes cited as holding membership, among them Bram Stoker, Sir Arthur Conan-Doyle, E. Wallis Budge and Eliphas Levi. Clearly none of these were actually part of the Order. It is also doubtful if the celebrated occult novelist Charles Williams was ever a member.

The title 'Golden Dawn', although usually referring to the entire organization, only applied to the first of three Orders within it. This first Order taught esoteric philosophy to the neophytes. The Second Order – the *Rosae Rubeae et Aureae Crucius* – taught scrying, astral travel and alchemy. It is important to note that only members of the Second Order were permitted to practice magic. Only a few of those who joined the Order ever rose to this stage. The Third order was presided over by the 'Secret Chiefs'. These supreme beings existed only upon the astral plane. They supposedly gave directives to the Chiefs within the Second Order, namely Mathers, Westcott and Woodman.

Howe has no doubt that Westcott's inspiration for the Chiefs was from Madame Blavatsky's *Mahatmas* – the Masters El Morya and Kuthumi. Blavatsky's desire to convey the messages of the 'Masters' was the *raison d'être* of the Theosophical Society. These 'Masters of Wisdom', or 'Mahatmas', were the rock upon which her philosophy stood. The belief that Blavatsky was communicating the wisdom of 'Masters' in her writings ensured her followers that her 'messages' owned certain potency.

Other organizations boasting guides from another realm existed. Karl von Eckartshausen wrote of a Secret Group of Spirits in *The Cloud Upon The Sanctuary* published in 1795. Dion Fortune speaks of the 'esoteric order', and Max Heindel, of the 'Elder Brothers'. In fact, contacts made on the inner planes were considered essential to a magical society. An 'esoteric' approach implies that knowledge, such as the wisdom of Masters, is known only to a minority. Always there exists an ambiance of secrecy, certain codes and keys being required to penetrate beyond deliberately obscure or misleading information to the truth.

The Golden Dawn was willing to provide instruction while also maintaining that those who were responsible for the teachings were in turn divinely inspired. The presence, or not, of the Mahatmas was a factor in Blavatsky's fall from grace. A very similar situation was to transpire when the Golden Dawn was beset by its own brand of calumny. Defining the existence and actual nature of The Chiefs was at the heart of one of the many disputes that befell the Order.

During the upheavals that were to follow some ten years later, much doubt was cast on the existence of the Secret Chiefs. From the beginning, Mathers was extremely reticent to discuss their nature. It was not until 1896, a time when his mental state is described by Howe as 'paranoid' that Mathers attempted to ratify his position. The following excerpt is from a manifesto circulated by him to the members of the Second Order. The salient points have been retrieved from a mass of verbiage.

> Concerning the Secret Chiefs of the Order...I can tell you *nothing*. I do not even know their earthly names. I know them only by certain secret mottoes. I have *but very rarely* seen them in the physical body...(in) my physical intercourse with them on these rare occasions...the effect produced...I can only compare...to the *continued* effect of that usually experienced momentarily by a person close to whom a flash of lightning passes...[19]

Insisting that only he was privy to intercourse with such exalted personages, Mathers then set out his terms. Only total obedience to his will would suffice! He pre-empted any opposition to this demand by producing his trump card.

> But unless the Chiefs are willing to give me the Knowledge, I cannot obtain it for you: – neither will I give it to you unless I know that the Order is being worked conformably with their wishes and instructions.[20]

By March 1890, the Golden Dawn could boast three active temples, The *Isis-Urania* in London, the *Osiris* in Weston-super-

Mare, and the *Horus* at Bradford. The London Order benefitted from Westcott's Masonic connections.

From the beginning, the ceremonies of Isis Urania were conducted at Mark Masons' Hall in Great Queen Street (now demolished) but members were careful not to embarrass the Masonic authorities, being told that they 'must not enter Mark Masons' Hall by the front door, but go under archway and down passage, entering by a door on the right'.[21]

Benjamin Cox, a member of the Rosicrucian Society in Bristol, was instrumental in the inauguration of the Weston-super-Mare Temple. Cox had known Westcott when he lived in nearby Martock in Somerset. The name 'Osiris' was chosen from a list compiled by Westcott – among the possible titles was 'Hermes', 'Minerva', and 'Thoth'. It seems significant that, at its inception, an Egyptian influence should be paramount in the Golden Dawn, Mathers feeling a strong affinity with this tradition. Initially, others appeared unified in this regard; however, the use of Egyptian magical workings was later to be at the centre of one of the many disputes that afflicted the Order. Unfortunately, when Cox died in 1895 the aspirations of the Temple at Weston-super-Mare went with him. The Horus Temple in Bradford (No.5) and the *Amen-Ra* in Edinburgh were to fare slightly better.

A few months before the opening of the first Temple a figure who was to play a leading role stepped upon the Golden Dawn stage. A dark, young woman, with a shock of curly hair and an intense look about the eyes, Moina Mathers (*nee* Mina Bergson) was said to be capable of mesmerising anyone she encountered. She was to have an overwhelming influence on the Golden Dawn, not only through being a modern Isis, but by demonstrating conclusively that women were quite capable of being practising magicians. Madame Blavatsky had demonstrated this power a decade earlier; now it was the turn of a 'modern woman'. Moina was to become an icon of modern magic. She would also outlive all three of the founders of the Golden Dawn.

II

Isis and Osiris

Woman is the magician born of Nature by reason of her great natural sensibility, and of her instructive sympathy with such subtle energies as these intelligent inhabitants of the air, the earth, fire, and water.
Moina Mathers

Mina Bergson's father was a Polish Jew who journeyed with his family to London in 1873. Her brother was Henri Bergson, the philosopher. He would be awarded the Nobel Prize in 1927. Henri had an original mind and wrote a treatise on humour – *Laughter – An essay on the meaning of the comic.* In an original aside he described the universe as 'a machine for making gods'.

Mina was a talented artist and awarded a scholarship to the Slade School of Art in 1883. There she met Annie Horniman who in the following years was to become a close associate. Eventually they would be fellow members of the Golden Dawn. Mina's spiritual path began to lead in the direction of the Order when in 1887 she met Mathers. The venue was the British Museum, where W.B. Yeats would also encounter him some years later. The mutual attraction of Mina Bergson and Samuel Mathers was both powerful and profound.

The couple were married on June 16th, 1890. The wedding took place at the church ministered by the Rev. William A. Ayton, one of the first initiates of the Golden Dawn. At that time he was certainly the oldest member of the Order. His motto was *Virtute Orta Occident Rarius* ('Those that rise by virtue rarely fall'). Yeats noted that he was, 'an old white-haired clergyman, the most panic-stricken person I have ever known'.[22]

The reason for his constant state of anxiety was put down to his involvement with magic. The old gentleman confided in Yeats that he had been much troubled throughout his life by his experiences with spirits and apparitions. He had always feared that the very act of perceiving them could lead to his being dominated by their powers. Ayton also claimed to have concocted the elixir of life in his alchemical laboratory. Upon further enquiry the old gentleman explained that the exercise was not as successful as it might have been. He had left the phial of precious liquid unopened for so long that the contents had completely evaporated.

Mina changed her name to Moina, which had more of a Celtic air about it. As Mary K. Greer observes, '...she went from being Mina Bergson, a Jewish art student, to being Moina Mathers, priestess of the Golden Dawn.'[23] Two years earlier, she had been the first initiate of the Isis-Urania Temple No.3. Initiated on the first of March, 1888, the day after her birthday, her motto was *Vestigial Nulla Retrorsum* ('I never retrace my steps'). On the same day, Mathers took two mottoes for himself – one Gaelic, the other in more conventional Latin. The first was *'S Rioghail Mo Dhream* ('Royal is my tribe'), the second, *Deo Duce Comite Ferro* ('God as my guide, the sword as my companion').

Mathers was always an opportunist, and he probably believed that he was marrying into money. If so, he had grossly misjudged the situation, and his succeeding involvement with Moina would be no sinecure. Poverty was to be his lot for most of his life, mainly through the mismanagement of his affairs. When he did acquire any funds he was often ridiculously extravagant. In the domestic sphere, however, he had shrewdly assessed that Moina would be loyal to his every whim. She did that and more, being absolutely devoted to her husband in every way, as well as sympathetic to his many and varied foibles.

Moina Mather's nature is an enigma. On the evidence of her artistic output, it seems she found it difficult to discipline herself. Her friend Annie Horniman was convinced that she had the promise to be a very great artist, a generous but far-fetched assessment. Any serious artistic ambitions she might have had were swiftly abandoned when she met her husband. She was transformed into the role of helpmate and a leading light in the Golden Dawn.

Mathers relied heavily on her ability to channel information during meditation. That Moina was a gifted psychic seems to be irrefutable. Her drawings, albeit fey, have the quality of one who is genuinely channelling the 'otherworld'. It is also to be suspected that she retreated into a world of daydreams and fantasies when she did not wish to look the real world in the eye. Dealing with Mathers irascible moods would no doubt have frequently prompted this involuntary withdrawal.

Her magical talents were prodigious and she was more than adequate at fulfilling the role of Priestess. Contemporary photographs of her performing the Rites of Isis, though impressive, probably do not do her justice. Her presence in these tableaux must have been quite stunning. She played the Priestess Anari to her husband's Ramses the Hierophant. It was in this role that she demonstrated how well she could play the role of the Dark Goddess.

Contemporary accounts of the Rites stress the inestimable contribution made by Moina. Some journalists went as far as to suggest that it was only her presence that prevented the performance from deteriorating into a farce. A correspondent from the *Sunday Chronicle* spoke of Moina as, 'invok(ing) Isis with …passion and force in both voice and gesture.'[24] There is enough evidence to make a strong case for Moina being 'the power behind the throne' in Mathers' marriage.

Very little biographical detail of Macgregor Mathers exists. Outwardly, he appears not to have been a particularly interesting character. Throughout his life, to compensate for his lack of worldly status, he nurtured a personal myth of owning aristocratic and specifically Celtic, connections. Moina persisted in keeping this pretence alive even after Mathers' death in 1919. In the preface to the 1926 edition of Mathers' work *The Kabbalah Unveiled*, she detailed her late husband's ancestry in an even more fantastic manner than he had ever done.

His ancestor, Ian MacGregor of Glenstrae, an ardent Jacobite, went over to France after the '45 Rebellion and under Lally Tolendal fought at Pondicherry. This ancestor was created Comte de Glenstrae by Louis XV. This French title was inherited by my husband and he always used it while living in France.[25]

From 1879 onwards Mathers felt this spurious pedigree entitled him to style himself the 'Comte de Glenstrae'. Frederick Holland, the occultist who gave Mathers his first instruction in the Qabalah, had no illusions about his pupil. Holland was a member of the Society of Rosicrucians and also the ill-fated *Society of Eight*, begun by Kenneth Mackenzie. In 1910 he wrote to Westcott concerning Mathers' supposedly exalted pedigree dismissing it as fantastical nonsense. Holland suggested that the family actually originated in Warwickshire!

To assess the man who eventually became the sole authority within the Golden Dawn, it is important to consider Mathers' motives at each stage of his career. This 'Monarch of the Glen', whose reign would end when his subjects rose up against him, was not obsessed with power for its own sake. While he was undeniably autocratic, his actions demonstrate that he was clearly also a seer. As Alan Richardson states, 'Westcott and most of the Order merely practised magic, but Mathers was a magician in every atom of his body...'[26] It was Mathers who provided *the form* of the magic propounded by the Golden Dawn; he wrote and conducted many of its rituals. When he knew that the end of his reign within the Order was imminent, the fabric of the Isis-Urania Temple was what he wished to preserve, even more than his own reputation.

Mathers' heart and soul were tied to magic; he could not envisage his life being any other way. We may condemn his self-centred and callous attitude to others, but we can only admire the dedication he showed towards his calling. We might make a comparison with Aleister Crowley whose behaviour was rarely beyond reproach. Yet Crowley also had a total dedication to magic, or 'magick' as he would have written the word. It is not always wise to judge our fellow men, particularly magicians. The inner and outer planes are separate and we are mistaken if we believe that one plane always exactly reflects the other.

Mathers believed that the path of the mystic and the path of the magician were separate. This division separates the Eastern school from the Western equivalent. The Eastern school seeks union with God; the Western school seeks to control the world by channelling Divine Will. Dion Fortune and W.G. Gray, committed followers of the Western Magical Tradition, would undoubtedly have sided with Mathers.

The two magicians mentioned also had more than an autocratic streak in their personality. However, neither has the reputation for being as despotic an individual as Mathers. Mathers became a tyrant and, like many before him, he was eventually deposed. Given the circumstances, it is difficult to imagine any other outcome. Mathers outraged the other members of the Order enough to have them unite and remove him from office in 1900. A few remained loyal to Mathers, but by 1903, the Golden Dawn, the order that he had helped to found, was no more.

Mathers' magical character is more paradoxical than most. The realm of the esoteric plays host to many an eccentric character, yet there must be some element of 'hearth magic' in the magician or he cannot survive. Magical teachers of the twentieth century, when offering advice to the initiate, would stress the importance of being engaged with ordinary domestic life. To retain a balance is essential on all the planes. The magician will bring about his own downfall if he cannot maintain this equilibrium. Mathers never learned this lesson. Although he was a great seer, he developed a tendency to use his powers to defend the indefensible in his behaviour. His actions became more extreme and in the end he retreated into a world of delusion.

His diet while he was living in Paris with Moina was one of radishes, washed down with copious quantities of brandy. Not even the hardiest constitution can survive on such a regime. Mathers' dilemna seems to have been one of being totally unable to deal with the mundane. Yeats confirms this when he speaks of Mathers as being a timeless figure, one not of this world.

> ...He was a necessary extravagance, and...in body and in voice at least he was perfect; so might Faust have looked in his changeless aged youth. In the credulity of our youth we secretly wondered if he had not met with, perhaps even been taught by, some old man who found the elixir.[27]

Yeats was only too aware of the dangers of rushing headlong into unknown worlds. Even a moment's consideration would have made any seeker upon Mathers' path hesitate – but he had no such qualms. His overweening arrogance convinced him he could be master of all on both the Inner and Outer Planes. Yeats' was applying his own considerable scholarship when he spoke of,

> ...that labyrinth that we are warned against in those *Oracles* which antiquity has attributed to Zoroaster, but modern scholarship to some Alexandrian poet: 'Stop not down to the darkly splendid world wherein lieth continually a faithless depth and Hades wrapped in cloud, delighting in unintelligible images'.[28]

Many quarrelled with Mathers, but few stood up to him. Westcott crumbled at the prospect of any confrontation with him. Annie Horniman permitted Mathers to take financial advantage of her for many years as we shall see later. Mathers possessed the kind of temperament that did not recognise the ability to debate or to compromise, as virtues. Once his mind was made up, it was impossible for him to alter his view. This tendency to deep-set convictions was his abiding fault. It did not help that Mathers was surrounded by sycophants a great deal of the time. Brodie-Innes, among others, constantly toadied to him, and as a result Mathers acquired a distorted view of his own importance.

The one who displayed the most loyalty to him was, of course, Moina who regarded her husband as myth, mystery and master all rolled into one. Iseult, daughter of Maud Gonne, spoke of Mathers in almost mythical terms. To her he was, 'a righter of wrongs, a chastiser of evildoers, a champion of the oppressed.'[29] His actions demonstrate that his character was anything other than noble and virtuous.

III

Pair of Priestesses

For she is the incarnation of the promise of perfection; the soul's assurance that, at the conclusion of its exile in a world of organized inadequacies, the bliss that once was known will be known again...
Joseph Campbell

The symbols often associated with the emancipated woman of the twentieth century are the bicycle, free love and universal suffrage. The imagery is inscribed indelibly upon any account of the 'Roaring Twenties' in America and the campaigns of Emily Pankhurst, the social reformer, in England. Her predecessor, the 'New Woman' as she was titled (whether with her approval or not) was regarded in 1887 as one who,

> ...goes everywhere, she does everything...(she is) a divinity in a ballroom...she drives a pair of horses like a charioteer... practices archery...(is) great at theatricals...designs, models and paints...none but herself can be her prototype.[30]

She was not, however, universally admired. A hostile reaction was particularly evident among those men who considered that women should not own independence. Opposition to the New Woman was strong, and a long and hard campaign would have to be fought before any real victory was gained. Two women who became notable members of the Golden Dawn were in their own particular way, at the forefront of this revolution. They were Annie Horniman and Florence Farr.

The grandfather of Annie Horniman gave his name to the famous company of tea importers. The passions of Annie's youth were the theatre and art. Annie, unlike Florence, could never be described as a vivacious character. In her youth she had the looks and air of the 'student swot'; in middle-age she became old-maidish and taciturn. Due to the success of the family business and various legacies that she received, Horniman quickly became a very rich young woman. In a material sense she was very fortunate. In other spheres of her life, probably those that she regarded as being more important to her, she was assuredly at a disadvantage.

Annie enrolled at the Slade School of Art on her twenty-second birthday. There she met Mina Bergson. The two became friends, and Annie was introduced to MacGregor Mathers in 1888. It is her relationship with the Mathers, and how her life revolved around them that gives us the key to Annie Horniman's character. She was extremely loyal to Moina, yet possessed an ambivalent attitude toward Mathers. This contradictory attitude would persist for the entire time she had any relationship with them.

Horniman became a member of the Golden Dawn in 1890, and took the motto, *Fortiter et Recte* ('Strength and Justice'). In the two years she had known Mathers, he had thoroughly instructed her in the art of astrology. Her dealings with this former tutor were a strange mixture of obsequiousness and respect. Much of the time while she was a member of the Order she unquestioningly obeyed Mathers' every directive. Even under extreme provocation, she rarely defended her own corner. Perhaps Mathers recognized in Horniman the perfect candidate for the role of his patron. It was a role she would willingly undertake for the next eight years or so.

At first, all went well. Through Annie's influence, the Mathers were employed as curators of the museum belonging to her father on the Horniman estate. The couple set up home at the estate lodge and began to conduct a kind of psychic salon. It was here that W.B. Yeats first visited them. The poet's relationship with the Mathers was to last as long as Horniman's, namely until the demise of the Golden Dawn.

During the years of her membership, Annie appears to have sublimated any emotional longings she might have had to the Order. In her writings in the Flying Rolls she refers to the Golden Dawn in the most high-flown terms.

> ...our Order is very dear, and we look back with real gratitude at those who watched us...and then brought us in to what has become a great and important part of our lives. In some cases it was an intimate friend....None of us who have made sacrifices for it in a right spirit are disappointed with the result...It is a gradual process, and often a painful one to experience, but well worth the sorrows to be borne...[31]

By 1893 she had attained the rank of Sub-Praemonstratrix and took her duties in the Order very seriously indeed. Horniman was responsible for ensuring that students were prepared for the examinations relating to their initiation. Annie would probably have been regarded as a 'bluestocking', a female intellectual whose preoccupations were cerebral rather than sensual. She never seemed to be at ease with men. Her attitude towards Mathers was unreal, and had elements of god-worship about it. Her closest friend in the Order, apart from Moina, was Florence Farr. In contrast to Annie, Florence exhibited an uninhibited longing to be admired by the male sex. She achieved this end quite naturally and with a minimum of Victorian artifice. Farr was a free, uninhibited spirit.

Annie possessed a resolute mind and quickly became skilled in the art of ritual. Realizing that any true magician should be able to successfully and competently practice magic, she was also aware of the trials that the magician must face, and was so much more than a mere occult pundit. Horniman expresses this succinctly herself.

If our Order be anything deeper and higher than a mere club for the dissemination of archaeological and literary knowledge, the obstacles to be overcome must be more subtle than those which come between us and success in the ordinary aims of life.[32]

Annie's sentiments were high-minded, with more than an echo of the schoolmistress, and there must have been many in the Order who regarded her as such. Her tendency, which increased through the years, was to rigidly adhere to systems; minute analysis was a defence against the release of her feelings. Her friendship with Florence Farr, although close at first, would inevitably flounder due to their marked difference in temperament.

Florence Farr had an unremarkable childhood, her only real interest like Annie, was in the theatre. She was described by Yeats, who was quite probably her lover at one time, as having 'a tranquil beauty' and 'a beautiful voice'. In contemporary photographs she displays an air of innocence combined with a languid sexuality. In her youth she achieved her ambition to become an actress, and in 1884 married a fellow actor – Edward Paget. The pair did not stay together very long and as soon as they separated Florence followed her own star.

Divorce, or indeed separation, was not common in the late Victorian era. Such behaviour carried enormous social stigma and the parties involved, particularly women, ran the risk of being ostracised from society. This was particularly prevalent among the middle classes who regarded respectability as a virtue to be prized above all others. It says a great deal for Florence Farr's sense of independence that she was prepared to flaunt convention, as she was to do much of her life.

Farr met W.B. Yeats through theatrical circles. He introduced her to Madame Blavatsky and to the Mathers. In 1890 she was initiated into the Golden Dawn. Her motto was *Sapientia Sapienti*

Dono Data ('Wisdom is a gift given to the wise'). The playwright Bernard Shaw, whose star was ascending at the time, seems to have spent an inordinate amount of time in her company. It seems they may have been romantically involved albeit briefly. Farr was keen to promote her career on the stage, and Shaw was delighted to have a performer with such dramatic presence to deliver his lines. He attempted to mould her personality offstage, but Farr was strong enough to resist his bullying ways. The picture painted of Shaw by Greer is of a disagreeable hypocrite and, by all accounts, one that is quite accurate.[33]

Farr's talents extended to music, singing while accompanying herself on various archaic stringed instruments which she played with a splendid sense of grace. With her taste for the theatrical, was well-suited to ritual magic. As she progressed in the Order she became its most talented female magician. Her writings upon magical theory are impressive and she also excelled in 'astral journeying'. Today this is a much debased term, one usurped by the vagaries of the New Age. In the context of the Golden Dawn, it was a practice conducted within strict discipline to develop the 'magical imagination'.

In 1893, Westcott resigned from the post of Praemonstratrix of The Isis-Urania Temple and Florence Farr was appointed in his place. The duties of this position included responsibility for all the rituals, invocations and teachings in the Order. She was also, in effect, Mathers' representative in England, as he had by this time departed for Paris. Farr became an excellent officer in the order, well-liked and respected by her juniors. Her only fault was a certain laxness in recording and ordering the day-to-day business of the Golden Dawn. This would have been in complete contrast to Westcott's clerical thoroughness. With his methods, the progress of initiates had been strictly monitored and filed away. Farr's temperament was not suited to such an approach, and this lack of method would have consequences in the future.

In 1894, Farr published a *novel a roman* entitled *The Dancing*

Faun. It was a thinly disguised account of her personal life. In its pages she lampooned Shaw's overbearing character and, as would be expected, championed the cause of the independent woman. Erudite, articulate and insightful, Farr lived the character she created on stage and in her pages. She had truly become an emancipated figure, one that represented a woman free of restrictions, both sexual and cultural.

In the nineteenth century, the deciphering of markings on the Rosetta Stone had excited a great many scholars. E. Wallis Budge's translation of a key text in the Book of the Dead had also stimulated many academics. Egypt held an overriding fascination for her Farr and she was intensely involved in initiating rituals once performed in Ancient Egypt. She had been able to incorporate the basic tenets of the Golden Dawn into her own group workings. By involving herself with the Egyptian pantheon and their magical methods, Farr believed that she was following the path of traditional magic and in this, she was correct.

By 1896, Farr had accumulated enough material to produce a book detailing her research. It was titled *Egyptian Magic: Occult Mysteries in Ancient Egypt*. Next to fascinate her was alchemy, and she produced a treatise – *Euphrates* – on this as well. She described its content as 'a study of the philosophy of nature and a guide to the attainment of perfection of mind and body – the achievement of Adeptship.'[34] Farr had gained that fundamental and indispensable insight into the nature of magic – the universe alone permits successful manifestation. As she wrote herself, 'If we labour against the World's Will we shall fail...'[35]

Farr had contacted an Egyptian woman during her astral meditations and, as a result, travelled to Paris in order to consult Mathers. She wished to make certain that he approved of her methods in overseeing the Isis-Urania Temple as well as discussing the Egyptian guide she had contacted. At their meeting, Mathers pronounced that the contact was, without doubt, a Secret Chief. This was a great admission on the part of Mathers, as he regarded contact with the Chiefs as exclusively his.

He then suggested a group should be formed within the Second Order to specifically work with this illustrious personage. Farr readily agreed, and the seeds of what was later to become the Sphere Group were sown. Annie Horniman was closely involved with Florence Farr's plans, and all went harmoniously with this inner group for many years.

Annie Horniman's magical aspirations were equally high. She too was working to discover an Egyptian figure with whom she might communicate. Farr's success in having contacted a 'Chief' may have inspired her. Her aim was to bond so strongly with this contact when it appeared that their life energies would be combined. Two candidates eventually appeared to her – *Nemkheftkah* and *Mut-em-menu*. Horniman was later convinced that she may have been either one in a previous incarnation. In celebration of her success Annie constructed a small wooden shrine for her personal rituals with these entities. This artefact was later decorated by Edmund Hunter, another Second Order member.

In 1897, Westcott left the Order completely. In subsequent contacts with other members he behaved as peremptorily as possible. The circumstances of his departure require a detailed exposition and they are discussed later. The significance of Westcott's decision upon Florence Farr's life was immense. Now, in addition to being Praemonstratrix, she was 'Chief Adept in Charge in Anglia'. Her duties were to supervise not only the Isis-Urania Temple, but also the three other Temples in Great Britain. She ranked second only to the Mathers in the Order. Her appointment seems logical, almost inevitable. In taking over all of Westcott's responsibilities and some of Horniman's also, she wielded an enormous power. It was inevitable that there would be those who wished to influence her, and others who simply envied her position. It is a credit to her resolution that she managed to maintain unity in the Order for the length of time she did.

IV

Rhymer and Revolutionary

...I began certain studies and experiences that were to convince me that images well up before the mind's eye from a deeper source than conscious or subconscious memory.
W.B. Yeats

Maud Gonne was the child of English parents and was raised for the greater part of her life in Protestant Ireland. Like Annie Horniman and Florence Farr, she had a penchant for the stage. A greater passion, for politics and intrigue, later enveloped her. The resulting combination of the dramatic and the revolutionary ensured that her life was never dull, but one that also full of tragedy.

She had an extraordinarily captivating presence, aided by her being six feet in height. The latest Paris gowns enhanced her looks even more, and she was regarded as a society beauty, rivalling even Lily Langtry and Lady Randolph Churchill. She even caught the eye of Edward VII, then Prince of Wales. It was rumoured that the future king wished her to be his mistress.

Maud Gonne's relationships with men were stormy, and often short-lived. It might be concluded that she preferred her love life to be that way. She was adored by a poet, and felt a great affinity with him. Together they journeyed to the pinnacles of the astral realms. Unfortunately, her taste in lovers did not include the kind of sensitive soul that he so obviously was. He played the role of confidant and close companion but it was a role he found only partially fulfilling. The man was, of course, William Butler Yeats, the greatest lyricist that Ireland ever produced.

Yeats was born in Dublin, but the city life never appealed to him as much as the rural haven to be found on the west coast of Ireland. As a child he was fascinated by the tales of fairy folk that he had heard among the country people in County Sligo. Later, in his eagerness for a greater knowledge of the mystical, Yeats began to read the magical writings of Paracelsus as well as those of Blake and Swedenborg. In 1885, he formed a 'Dublin Hermetic Order' with George Russell. The latter, known as 'A.E.', became celebrated as a poet and painter in his own right as well as being a lifelong friend of Yeats.

Russell was a visionary of extraordinary powers. From his youth he gained much inspiration and joy from the natural world in a manner similar to the romantic painter Samuel Palmer. Palmer encouraged contemplation of the world with a new eye. Russell, agreeing, believed that in this way man would step through the veil of illusion and experience a new existence. It was the creed of an advanced and enlightened soul. He advocated setting aside the sphere of reason and wholly embracing the natural intuition that resides within us all.

When we turn from books to living nature we begin to understand the ancient wisdom, and it is no longer an abstraction, for the great spirit whose home is in the vast becomes for us a moving glamour in the heavens, a dropping tenderness in the twilight, a visionary light in the hills, a voice in the heart. The earth underfoot becomes sacred and the air we breathe is like wine poured out for us by some heavenly cupbearer.[36]

We may have A.E. to thank for being the catalyst that inspired Yeats' own poetic vision. It may have also spurred his involvement with magic and mysticism, an interest that was to remain with him for the rest of his life. Russell told Yeats of his own experience when he felt,

'a steady light in the brain...revealed in ecstasy of thought or power in speech and in a continuous welling up from within myself of intellectual energy, vision or imagination.[37]

In 1887, Yeats' family moved to London. 'Willie' was then twenty-two. He set about joining the Theosophical Society and met its founder, Madame Blavatsky. Now in her last years, this formidable lady was ensconced in Upper Norwood, a far-flung suburb of London. In the confines of a cottage owned by Mabel Collins – the occult novelist – the poet and the wise woman surveyed each other. Later Yeats would describe Blavatsky as, 'a sort of old Irish peasant woman with an air of humour and an audacious power.'

Apparently Madame took a liking to him, to the extent of inviting Yeats to become a member of her 'Inner Sanctum'. It was to be an uneasy relationship and after a short time he was, 'with great politeness…asked to resign.' During his brief sojourn in her company, Blavatsky had expounded to Yeats upon 'the serpent power'. Yeats would later refer to her as 'a pythoness'. 'Willie' introduced Maud Gonne to Blavatsky in 1890. She described the Theosophist as, 'a strange, interesting figure with big pale luminous eyes in a large yellow face.'[38]

Yeats was making his first faltering steps along the mystical path and was ripe for a mentor. The die was cast when he first encountered Mathers in the British Museum in 1888. Already the author of *The Kabbalah Unveiled*, Mathers impressed Yeats greatly with his occult knowledge and obvious devotion to magic. The two often met at Forrest Hill where Mathers was living with Moina. In Yeats, Mathers recognised a natural medium and set about invoking visions in the poet's receptive mind. In his *Autobiographies* Yeats describes his first encounter with the magical planes.

…there rose before me mental images that I could not control: a desert, and a black Titan raising himself up by his two hands from the middle of a heap of ancient ruins.[39]

The following year, 1889, Yeats was fated to meet the woman who he would love for the greater part of his life. From her point of view, Maud Gonne's first impression of this devoted admirer is hardly the stuff of romance. She described him as,

> ...a tall lanky boy with deep set dark eyes behind glasses, over
> which a lock of dark hair was constantly falling, to be pushed
> back impatiently by long sensitive fingers...stained with paint
> – dressed in shabby clothes.[40]

Their relationship was to be almost exclusively cerebral rather
than physical, although Yeats desperately wished otherwise.
Such an unrequited sexual situation, brimming with frustration
is somehow typical of the darker Victorian byways.

The Golden Dawn, being a progressive institution, we might
expect to be sexually liberated. The accounts of the Order that we
have tell a different story. With a few notable exceptions, the
Golden Dawn was as much subject to late-Victorian morals as the
rest of society. The soubriquet 'Naughty Nineties' did not apply
in the hallowed surrounds of the Isis-Urania Temple. The
prospect of sex might have hovered over some of the exchanges
between the men and women of the Order, yet it was entirely
unfulfilled. There were those who abhorred sex, such as Mathers
and his wife, those indifferent to sex, such as Annie Horniman,
and those who were obsessed by it, such as Crowley and Dr.
Berridge (as we shall hear later).

Yeats joined the Golden Dawn in 1890. His motto was *Demon
est Deus Inversus* ('The Devil is the converse of God'). The choice
of motto is interesting as it reflects Yeats' philosophy of the time.
He still embraced a Christian notion of duality with regard to
questions of 'good' and 'evil'. Yeats even implied, when writing
to his close friend and artist W.T. Horton, that the Golden Dawn
wholly embraced Christianity.

> ...Nor is our order anti-Christian. That very pentagram which
> I suggested your using is itself as you would have learned, a
> symbol of Christ...[41]

Regrettably, Horton's own experiences with the Golden Dawn would turn out to be brief and unhappy. He was a notoriously neurotic individual, beset by guilt caused probably by sexual inadequacy, far too much the prey to his own vacillating intellect to take up magic.

Yeats introduced Maud Gonne to the Mathers the next year. After an intense séance, perhaps in their company, she reflected upon whether to join the Order. She was enthusiastic, and became a member in 1891. She chose as her motto *Per Ignum Ad Lucem* ('Through fire to the light'). Yeats was obviously excited at having his muse close to him in the Order. Gonne for her part was impressed only with the leading lights in the Golden Dawn – Moina, Florence Farr, Algernon Blackwood, and J. Brodie-Innes. The company of the rest did not appeal to her at all. Yeats, who secretly hoped Maud Gonne would soon be his bride, encouraged her to develop her psychic qualities as much as possible.

It cannot be claimed that Maud Gonne was ever a major player in the Order. She did not have the discipline for taking part in ritual and was thus by definition excluded from the path of the adept. Although drawn towards clairvoyance, much of her mediumship was spurious. Its content was generally a hodge-podge of wild imaginings prompted by Catholic guilt. Too often morbid fantasies invaded her unconscious. She appeared to be either unable to dismiss them, or only too willing to indulge their presence.

Maud Gonne was a figure too much wrapped up in her own personality and prestige. Although one can never doubt her sincerity, passion often clouded her judgment. Political change, of the most extreme kind, was what fired her soul, and such a doctrine determined everything she did. She was almost fatally attracted to radicals and revolutionaries, while Yeats' sensitivities were repelled by them.

In 1894, Gonne left the Golden Dawn. She gave as her reason

that she believed it was aligned to Freemasonry which she opposed for political reasons. Although Yeats attempted to convince her this was not so, she was adamant. Her belief that '...Free Masonry, as we Irish know it, is a British institution and has always been used politically to support the British Empire', sealed her decision. The use of the term 'we Irish' is astonishing. Maud Gonne was not Irish, being born in Aldershot of an English mother and father. She passionately championed the poor of Ireland, which can only be seen as laudable, but in the matter of her birth she was deluded. Gonne, tethered to her own histrionics, let the smoke of her fiery demeanour blind her vision.

Even after her resignation from the Order, she remained on friendly terms with the Mathers and continued to visit them in Paris. She was somewhat scathing about Mathers' pretensions to Celtic aristocracy. Writing in her autobiography, she recalled that,

> Pretenders to thrones were as plentiful in Paris at that time as the blackberries in the fields of Howth of my childhood. Even Willie Yeats' friend McGregor [sic], the famous occultist, I think had a throne-pretender for Scotland up his sleeve, whether on the terrestrial plane or astral plane, I don't quite remember.[42]

The sensual nature that accompanies altered states also excited Gonne, and she imbibed hashish with Yeats. She may well have also experimented with chloroform and mescaline. Having turned her back on the training in mysticism offered by the Golden Dawn, Maud had become a loose cannon. Accounts of her visions are vivid and filled with Gaelic imagery, but they are mainly constructed from conscious ideas that she gathered from reading. Yeats' plan, that they might found a Celtic Order together perhaps with Mathers help, was merely 'smoke in a bottle' as the Irish themselves are prone to say.

In 1903, Maud Gonne adopted the Catholic faith. Three days later she married the arch Fenian, John MacBride. The marriage was to be short-lived. It was quickly revealed that her husband was a violent, irresponsible drunk. Gonne parted from him within a matter of months and had little to do with him thereafter. He was later to be executed by the British government for his part in the Easter Uprising of 1916. So much for Gonne's nationalist dream for Ireland – yet another episode doomed to go the way of all her dreams. Her paradoxical nature almost guaranteed that tragedy and disappointment would be her lot. Her son-in-law, Francis Stuart, described Gonne in less than glowing terms as one,

> ...who fastened on causes as an outlet for her passions which weren't fulfilled through the senses...(someone who) found in nationalist passion an emotion to fill the void.[43]

The only constant throughout Maud's life was Yeats. Whether through perversity or pragmatism, she continually rejected his proposals of marriage. His love for her constantly drove him to despair, though this spurning of him may have inspired some of his finest poetry. That the pair had a spiritual bond seems unquestionable. Their relationship could be seen as that of priest and priestess, but that would be stretching the notion to the limit. Whether Yeats himself was ever wholly committed to the Golden Dawn is also debatable. One suspects that his eclectic personality regarded all their magical goings-on as merely grist to his creative mill.

That said, there is a case for the opposite view. Yeats did work hard within The Inner Order – all his tools and talismans are on display in Dublin University – and he did write the following:

> Now as to magic. It is surely absurd to hold me "weak" or otherwise because I choose to persist in a study which I

decided deliberately four or five years ago to make, next to my poetry, the most important pursuit of my life...If I had not made magic my constant study I could not have written a single word of my Blake book, nor would The Countess Kathleen have ever come to exist. The mystical life is the centre of all that I do and all that I think and all that I write.[44]

Perhaps the most bizarre episode in the relationship of Maud and Willie centres about the last proposal of marriage that Yeats made to her. With the death of MacBride she was a widow in 1916, and Yeats did not hesitate to pledge his troth. As before, Gonne refused him. Undaunted, the rejected suitor asked if he might have permission to court her daughter Iseult! The response of the mother is not recorded but it seems Yeats was determined to pursue her child.

Of this rather tasteless episode, the twenty-three-year-old Iseult wrote to her friend, 'Thirty years difference is...a little too much...I said *No* and it didn't seem to affect him much...' A few days later the indefatigable Yeats made yet another proposal of marriage, this time to Georgie Hyde-Lees, a woman only three years older than Iseult. She, on the other hand, accepted. Little is known of their life together but it was always said that the marriage was very fulfilling for both parties. Yeats' final experiment in mysticism incorporated his wife's supposed psychic talents and will be discussed later.

We must now return to an earlier period, and examine Yeats' progress within the Golden Dawn. At some time after 1892, he succeeded in passing the elemental grades, and attained the first part of the Degree of *Theoricus Adeptus* in 1895. It was not until 1912 that he completed this qualification, at a time when the Golden Dawn, in its original incarnation, no longer existed. Consequently, Yeats had thrown in his lot with the *Stella Matutina*, the offshoot of the Order that was briefly under the stewardship of Brodie-Innes, before passing to Felkin. The former then returned to the Mathers fold.

It seems that Yeats had always had his own views on the grading system of the Order. For him, the Sphere of Tiphareth was the highest point of initiation. He appeared to still hold this view in 1901 and even later, when he was attempting to lead the Golden Dawn. By 1914, Yeats was seeking to attain the level of Geburah, making him an *Adeptus Major*, rather than *Adeptus Minor*. This would have made him a member of the Second Order, according to the revised system. Yeats was not involved in any further examinations, but after undergoing the Portal Ritual in January of 1903, he was received into the Inner Order. It is not easy to assess whether he continued to participate in ritual magic at all, though it seems only moderately likely.

The friendship of Mathers and Yeats never ceased to be anything but all-embracing. In one as suspicious as Mathers, a man who demanded total loyalty if not subservience from his fellow beings, it is extraordinary that their intimacy flourished. He seemed to have trusted Yeats more than any other member of the Order, hindsight indicating that he may have had good reasons for this. Mathers was later to have a brief alliance with another member of the Order, Aleister Crowley. The 'Great Beast' later viciously satirised him as the nauseous character 'Douglas' in his novel *Moonchild*.[45] Yeats was also satirised in the same work as the inept 'Gates'.

Yeats was obviously inspired by Mathers. Their friendship appeared to spur a broadening of his poetic vision. A new dimension of meaning and rich imagery appeared in Yeats' work during the period from 1890 to 1900. This entry from a notebook of 1915 for a proposed ritual, shows that the years with Mathers had brought any number of transcendental themes to the poet:

It is time to be done with it all
The stars call and all the planets
And the purging fire of the moon

And yonder in the cold silence of cleansing night
May the dawn break and gates of day be set wide open.

Yeats made several visits to Paris in the 1890s. He was in a state of turmoil, prompted as always by his unreciprocated love for Maud Gonne. Yeats was also involved with another woman – Diane Vernon. His inability to return the love she offered him made the poet even more desolate and despondent. Yeats became dissipated in his habits, taking hashish and drinking to excess.

This all seems to be another pose, however, such dissolute behaviour consciously aping the 'decadents'. This group of artists, poets and writers were supposed to reflect the dark side of the 'Naughty Nineties'. Those, who like Symonds and Baudelaire brought about their own end as a result of their excesses, were heroes among young aesthetes of the time. Yeats, to his credit, always managed to maintain a vision that embraced more joyous horizons.

When Yeats visited the Mathers in Paris in 1894, two years after they had moved to the city, their mutual friendship was in its infancy. This rather whimsical account of an evening with Yeats and the Mathers is provided by Joseph Hone, Yeats' official biographer.

Mathers was a gay and companionable man. In the evenings he made his wife and Yeats play chess with him, a curious form of chess with four players. Yeats' partner was Mrs. Mathers, Mathers' (was) a spirit. Mathers would shade his eyes with his hands and gaze at the empty chair at the opposite corner of the board before moving his partner's piece.[46]

Whatever else transpired during their meetings, when Yeats returned to Ireland he was prompted to practice a mild variety of magic himself. He spent the summer of 1894 with his Uncle George Pollexfen in Sligo, and during this time Yeats introduced his receptive relative to astrology and thought transference. Yeats even cured his uncle of a delirium while he was in high fever. He invoked the Archangel Gabriel to bring the sufferer healing through the element of water.

In 1896, Yeats once more returned to Paris. His great ambition at that time was to found 'The Order of Celtic Mysteries' within The Golden Dawn. Yeats' vision was for an Ireland that embraced the beliefs of the ancient world, combined with a faith relevant to modern times. As so often with Yeats, his intentions fell between two stools. His idiosyncratic ideas of 'religion' would never have gained the approval of the Catholic Church, and his nationalism was too archaic and insubstantial for the Fenian movement. In his enthusiasm, Yeats had not considered that others might not be so afire with his own ideas, often marked by a lyrical idiosyncrasy.

He had pictured in great detail how the new order would be, and had even chosen a symbol for the new Order – The Hare. A location for the new order's activities, on Lough Key in Roscommon had been found. There was a ruined castle – the ideal setting for him and Mathers to perform rituals to the Celtic gods and goddesses. To Maud Gonne, Yeats described his 'Castle of Heroes'. He also endeavoured to enthuse Florence Farr with his schemes. She spent much time with him at this point in his life, and enthusiastically described Yeats' vision for the new order as the joining of 'the Supernal and the Terrestrial natures'.

Yeats was convinced that Mathers would be sympathetic to the idea of a union between the Celtic and Egyptian pantheon. He was convinced that a bond existed through their both having an intrinsic earthiness. He was greatly disappointed when Mathers refused to commit himself to the proposal. We can only speculate that Mathers' was distracted by increasingly tenuous hold upon the Golden Dawn. It was in this year that the Mathers quarrelled badly with Annie Horniman, an episode we will examine in some detail later.

In his poem *Images* (known only in a draft version and never published), Yeats seems to be hovering between a spiritual path and his own taste for the poetry of passion. The narrator of the poem appears undecided as to the direction he must follow. The extract, probably written in the late 1920s, is Yeats looking back on these often confused years. He captures a time when he saw himself as being in a halfway house between transcendence and misery.

> But the wind changes and the valley howls
> One howls his answer back and one by one
> They drop upon all fours, creep valley-wards
> Question that instant for these forms O heart
> These chuckling & howling forms begot the sages

Yeats' turmoil was mild compared to Mathers' rapid descent into a world of fantasy. His mind was whirling, caught in a vortex with its centre in his assumed Celtic past. An alarming picture of Mathers' persona in the closing years of the nineteenth century is painted by Yeats. At this point he appears to have changed his mind and warmed to Yeats' idea of the Celtic Order. However, the instigator himself appears to have grave doubts as to whether Mathers should be involved in the scheme at all.

> MacGregor himself lived in a world of phantoms...The break up of his character that was soon to bring his expulsion from my order had begun. He was slowly demoralised by the Celtic Movement. As Sir Walter Scott, he had taken to wearing highland costume though he had I believe never been in the highlands...He called every young man 'lad' and drank much brandy...He wished to play some part in the manner of Rob Roy and dreamt of the restoration of the Stuarts to some highland kingdom.[47]

With the turn of the century, Yeats' own interest in the Celtic Movement died. Ostensibly, he became more involved in a political solution for Ireland's problems. Submitting to the wiles of Maud Gonne, he joined the Irish Republican Brotherhood. A police report of 1899 described Yeats as 'more or less revolutionary', a verdict which was more apposite than it might appear. Yeats had never been convinced of an exclusively political remedy for Ireland. The spiritual side of his character preferred to believe that changing the consciousness of her people would have a more of a positive result. It was on this point that he and Maud Gonne were ever divided.

With the Golden Dawn in some disarray from 1900 onwards, Yeats, always the idealist, saw himself as its saviour. He decided to establish 'a perfectly honest Order, with no false mystery' with himself at its head. In the Spring of that year Yeats wrote to Lady Gregory, his artistic patron, explaining the onerous nature of his task.

> The trouble is that my Cabalists are hopelessly unbusiness-like, and their minutes and the like are in complete confusion. I have had to take the whole responsibility for everything, and to decide on every step. I am hopeful of the result...I arraigned Mathers on Saturday last before a chapter of the Order. I was carefully polite...the honour one owes to a fallen idol. Whatever happens the activities of the society will have nothing unworthy to pass down to posterity.[48]

Whether Yeats realised what it actually meant to be the leader of the Golden Dawn is questionable. Although he relished the idea of dressing up in magical garb and acting a part, he was definitely not suited to run a magical society. Too much of the free spirit was in his nature. He did, however, take it upon himself to assume control of the Second Order, and became Imperator of the Isis-Urania Temple Outer Order also. He quickly realized that attempts on his part to restore any unity were in vain.

With all this furore, Yeats' relationship with Mathers took a turn for the worse. Mathers always preferred to sunder a friendship rather than admit that he might actually have been wrong. He wrote to Yeats informing him that he was, 'associating with a set of rascally thieves'. He went on to berate him for 'betray[ing] your country to the Saxons'. Mathers' strictures turned out to be irrelevant to Yeats' standing in the Order. The result of some political machinations between Annie Horniman and Brodie-Innes was that Yeats was abandoned on the sidelines. He was deprived of his rank and thus was left powerless in the Order.

At this time Yeats still strongly believed in the existence of the Secret Chiefs. This is shown in an extract from his paper – *Is the Order of the R.R.et A.C to remain A Magical Order?*

...the stream of lightning is awakened in the Order, and the Adepti of the Third Order and of the Higher Degrees of the Second Order [are] summoned to our help.[49]

In 1912, he attained the grade of *Theocritus Adeptus Minor* but was then disinclined to involve himself any further with the activities of the Golden Dawn, or any other magical society. He still seemed to be on good terms with both Westcott and Dr. Felkin, a member who had risen in the ranks. However, by 1919 the latter was censorious of Yeats saying that he 'talked too freely of the Order' in America. In 1922, Yeats proclaimed that the Golden Dawn had 'ended amid quarrels caused by men, otherwise worthy, who claimed a Rosicrucian sanction for their fantasies'. He then left the Order for good.

Yeats' poem 'All Souls Night', written at Oxford in 1920, paints a more rounded picture of his old friend Mathers, who had died the previous year. The poem is partly a debate upon the alienation that personal vision may bring – a separation from the company of companions. The relevant lines are,

And I call upon MacGregor from the grave,
For in my first hard springtime we were friends,
Although of late estranged.
I thought him half a lunatic, half knave,
And told him so, but friendship never ends;

Also,

He had much industry at setting out,
Much boisterous courage, before loneliness
Had driven him crazed,
For meditations upon unknown thought
Make human intercourse grow less and less;

The influence of the Golden Dawn teachings upon Yeats' philosophy is reflected in his later *Visions*. This volume consists of a personal system of magical correspondences, combined with various Qabalistic overtones. Like many who attempt to fit existing systems into their own schemes, the Qabalah refused to oblige for Yeats. The book has remained a mere curiosity ever since, finding only a readership with the most devoted of the poet's admirers. By 1924, Yeats had abandoned all occult systems describing them as 'an aberration'.

His only venture into the esoteric was to conduct sessions of 'automatic writing' with Georgie, the wife he had taken in 1917. Mathers would not have approved of all this; the notion of surrendering the will to outside influences other than the directives of the Chiefs, would have been anathema to his own magical principles.

Parisian Exile

'A strong and decided will can, in a short space of time arrive at absolute independence.'
Eliphas Levi

In 1893, the *Amen-Ra* Temple was consecrated in Edinburgh. More significant however was Mathers' decision to set up a new Temple in Paris – *Ahathor*. It was to be numbered 7 in his scheme. Mathers announced that the Secret Chiefs had informed him this should be located in Paris, and this was where he was meant to be. Mathers' real motive for leaving England is not easy to discover. It may have been that he felt drawn to the occult tradition as it had always been practised in France, or he felt stifled by England. More pragmatically, perhaps he believed he and Moina could live more cheaply in Paris.

Whatever his thinking, in order to finance a move to France and set up a Temple, funds would obviously be required. Mathers must have discussed this with Moina, but in his own mind it was all a *fait accompli*. Mathers more or less left Moina to the task of coercing Horniman to comply with his wishes. At this point Moina's attitude to her friend Annie, already disingenuous, began to involve a certain deceit. Initially, she may not have intended to be devious, but her loyalty to Mathers outweighed any other moral consideration.

Much had occurred in the previous two years with regard to her relationship with Annie. Mathers had fallen out with Annie's father early in 1891 and the couple had quit the estate. Since then, they had been living cheaply in lodgings off the Tottenham Court Road in London.

Horniman's hopes for Moina's destiny begin to emerge. She

was convinced that her friend's artistic talents were becoming atrophied. What was she doing wasting her time following Mathers around as his priestess? She was determined that Moina should be sent to Paris to develop her talents as a painter. This was Horniman's intention when she gave Moina various sums of money, totalling more than £100.[50] Moina established herself in a studio in Paris. Mathers, supposedly following the dictum of the Secret Chiefs, joined her almost immediately. With his arrival, Moina's artistic career effectively ceased. This turn of events must have greatly strained Horniman's loyalty.

Mathers had already made plans as to how he would occupy himself in Paris. He knew that the Parisian libraries held more ancient magical texts than the equivalent in London. Translating them would provide him with an income. Mathers was also convinced that Henri Bergson, Moina's unmarried brother, would help to support the couple. In this he was mistaken, and it seems unlikely that any money was ever forthcoming from that source.

Subsequently, Annie Horniman agreed to give the Mathers a stipend of £200 a year. Mathers assured Annie that within two years they would have acquired enough capital to be able to purchase their own property in Paris. Did Horniman really believe that this would happen? It is possible that she felt her position in the Golden Dawn was always uncertain and she could only gain any security by handing over her cash. Whatever the reason for her largesse, it seems a foolhardy gesture.

The Ahathor Temple in Paris recruited eleven members during its tenure. In 1895, Gerard Encausse, more widely known in esoteric circles as 'Papus', was admitted to the Order, perhaps in an honorary capacity. Papus is remembered for being the founder of the Martinist Order and the author of *The Tarot of the Bohemians*. A devotee of Eliphas Levi, he was a member of both the Theosophical Society and the Freemasons for a short period in his life. With the turn of the century, Temples were set up in various locations in New Zealand and in America. Certainly there was a great deal of activity in New York, and possibly lodges were set up in Boston, Philadelphia and Chicago, albeit briefly.

Mathers believed that by increasing his own understanding of magic he would proportionately increase his personal power. In this he may have been right, but he did not realise the toll his involvement in all this would take upon his personality. Mathers proposed to work upon one of the foremost and most ancient sources of arcane knowledge that existed. This came in the form of a 'grimoire' – the word is a corruption of grammar i.e. method. There are many such works, and the majority are valueless, consisting of spells, feeble invocations, and a ragbag of magical correspondences.

Already, Mathers had experience of translating one of the few worthwhile examples. In 1888, he had published *The Key of Solomon the King*. It is a fascinating work and of value to any student of magic and magical history. The 1972 edition has an introduction by Richard Cavendish which includes this succinct observation:

> ...the demons, or 'animals of darkness' as the key calls them, are forces from within the magician, as dwellers in the infernal abyss of his own inner core. [51]

Broadly, magic relies for success on two methods. Moses Maimonides the Jewish philosopher of the Middle Ages was perhaps the first scholar to delineate the difference between 'natural' and demonic magic. His definition still holds good. The former method embodies the theory of 'correspondences', the belief that an action performed in one location results in a desired effect somewhere else. This is often referred to as 'sympathetic magic' and has its origins in ancient practices. An obvious example might be the 'rain dances' of the Native Americans, or a shaman donning the skin of an animal that the community desires to hunt. This is the sphere of 'invocation' in the magical world.

The second method is the 'evocation' of spirits. Once these appear the magician orders these supernatural beings to do his will. This method obviously has many obvious dangers. It is certainly a procedure that cannot be recommended by any responsible teacher of magic, or any writer upon the subject. Apologists stress that angels not demons are the agency of manifestation and, being the messengers of God, they may be trusted. Common sense indicates this is a gamble with very long odds.

The Judaic tradition specifically warns against magical practices, claiming that all knowledge of magic was transmitted by angels who 'fell from heaven'. The implication is that no self-respecting angel appears during a ritual. That however may easily be disputed, as the four archangels – Raphael, Michael, Gabriel and Uriel represent the four directions (respectively East, South, West and North) in many *bona fide* rituals.

Mathers would have been an accomplished sorcerer in any era, but he was venturing into territory that was unfamiliar. The suggestion that he was likely to be on treacherous ground simply because he over-estimated his own powers is also valid. 'Pride comes before a fall' is an old adage and a sure one. In the popular imagination, evoking spirits will forever be associated with necromancy and diabolism and with good reason. Mathers himself was not so blind that he was not aware of the odour of 'black magic' that hung over the grimoires. For this reason he apparently, 'removed one or two experiments'.[52]

The Key is a comprehensive instruction book for the under-taking of magical rituals although the amount of preparation for these proceedings is incredibly lengthy. Not only must the day, hour and phase of the moon be adhered to for the ritual to be effective, but also the sign of the zodiac that the lunar body occupies. Demons may only be evoked at night as they are creatures of the darkness. There must be no wind, and the correct pentacle must be made, consecrated at the appropriate time, and worn by the magician. The angels of the Sephiroth are called upon, and the practioner must be clothed in white leather, linen and silk. He is warned that his conjuration of spirits will not always be successful. If this is so, 'stronger and more potent' conjurations are given, and even an 'extremely powerful' version if all else fails. To cause the demons to depart, the entire first chapter of Genesis must be recited! A fatiguing process one would imagine.

In *The Key* , besides the usual curses, love philtres and charms, there are instructions for making a magic carpet. Also mentioned is a magic girdle, to enable the wearer to run at great speeds. A formula that will bestow the ability to cause an earthquake is the most dramatic offering. The six months of purification preceding rituals and other exhausting and alienating processes involved, almost guarantee no modern magician would consider it worthwhile to embark on such tasks. If Mathers attempted to perform these rituals, which seems likely, then his dedication to magic was probably unmatched by any practioner of that era except Crowley.

And thus, emboldened by what he considered to be the successful venture of translating *The Key*, Mathers embarked on his new project. He proposed to translate the work that many occultists believed to be the most significant magical treatise in existence. This most celebrated of ancient texts is commonly known as *The Book of Abra-Melin the Magi*. It is the tale of an Egyptian Mage, one supposedly compiled by Rabi Yaakov Moelin in the fourteenth century.

Some controversy exists concerning its Jewish provenance, scholars suggesting that the work is nothing more than the French text of a collection of Medieval grimoires. Others insist that the French version is a poor cousin of the original, which totals four books. Mathers had managed to acquire a text that contained three. He was forced in the course of this work to translate a great deal of execrable French, and his task cannot have been made any easier by the text apparently being full of errors.

Mathers' version of *The Book of The Sacred Magic of Abra-Melin* was published at the end of the 1890s. In the introduction, he presents a comprehensive history of 'Abraham the Jew'. To cite the following passage,

> ...however much the life of a hermit or anchorite may appear to be advocated, we rarely, if ever find it followed by those Adepts whom I may perhaps call the initiated and wonder-working medium between the Great Concealed Adepts and the Outer World.[53]

There is no doubt that Mathers believed himself to be among 'the initiated'. He felt a kinship with Abraham as one who was wholly dedicated to the hermetic life. Apart from a *salon* that Mathers convened at his apartment in later years, he was essentially a recluse. He advocates that the 'Adept' cannot gain wisdom unless he practices a solitary mode of life. Mathers may have a point; the great occultists were, in the main, men of a retiring nature who closed themselves off from the hustle and bustle of the world.

In his translation, Mathers is at some pains to indicate that the whole of Abraham's work is based on the Qabalah. He is not above recommending his own work – *Kabbalah Unveiled* – on the subject. Mathers also advances his own theory that the basis of the Qabalah resides in the teachings of Ancient Egypt. Did he perform the rituals contained in the *Abra-Melin* treatise? In the introduction he describes the work as, 'an assemblage of directions for the production of Magical effects, which the Author of the book affirms to have tried with success.' [54] Is he referring to himself or the original author? In the final analysis it does not matter, as the outcome was that the Abra-Melin book did have a profound, and it must be said deleterious, affect on Mathers.

The text of the original German version describes an elaborate ritual to acquaint the magician with his 'guardian angel'. The preparation alone is estimated at taking up eighteen months, while Mathers insists that six months is sufficient. When the period of abstention and restriction has been completed, the Holy Guardian Angel will appear. Following that, the evocation of many demons and spirits is conducted. Of the former, these are Lucifer, Satan, Leviathan, Belial and various other notable members of the aristocracy of Hell. The rewards for this exercise are again typical of the promises made by all grimoires – the finding of treasure, love charms, magical flight and invisibility. In his preface, Mathers makes various comments on the efficacy of the work. He accepts the claim that 'Abraham the Jew' obtained a wife and a treasure of three million golden florins as a result of practicing this particular set of rituals.

Once more, Mathers also assuages his conscience regarding any suggestion that 'black magic' might be involved in all this. He deftly argues that the Abra Melin system is aligned to 'White' Egyptian magic rather than 'Black' Chaldean magic. Mathers reasons that when practising Egyptian magic the god forms are assumed by the magician, who then calls on the gods to control them. He deems this to be a very different process from simply evoking the gods and argues that this is the same method used in the Abra Melin System. Mathers was clearly toying with very potent forces and for him to believe that he had minimized this power seems hopelessly optimistic. Had Mathers convinced himself he had the ability to control the universe?

Rather touchingly, he advocates the greatest courtesy when dealing with any infernal powers.

...it is only when they are obstinate and recalcitrant that severer measures should be resorted to; and even with the Devils we should not *reproach them for their condition*...[55]

Did Mathers' dealings with the denizens of the infernal regions contribute to his ultimate downfall? Aleister Crowley, no stranger to demons himself, offered these comments:

> It is...always easy to call up the demons, for they are always calling you; and you have only to step down to their level and fraternize with them. They will then tear you in pieces at their leisure.[56]

Crowley clearly felt Mathers had *not* been able to control these dark powers and later in the same text he describes Anthony of Padua and Mathers as victims of 'demonic possession'. Crowley asserts that he, on the other hand, successfully completed the Abra-Melin operation himself, once in China and again in Paris. Far from resulting in any Faustian pact, he felt he gained great wisdom from performing the ritual. The philosophy of Thelema, the revealing of his Holy Guardian Angel, and the dictation of the Book of the Law were, according to Crowley, the fruits of this experiment.

It is clear that during Mathers' attempts to translate the *Book of Abra-Melin* he suffered several bizarre experiences. Crowley warned him that working with the Abra-Melin manuscript was like 'handling dynamite'. The magical consensus seemed to be that copying the magic squares and sigils had the effect of releasing untrammelled energies. Although trivial in isolation, when considered together, several incidents Mather experienced amounted to a run of extraordinary ill-fortune. He had several accidents on his bicycle while commuting to the Arsenal Library, and then lost a large portion of the manuscript and his notebooks. Furthermore, during this time the Mathers were in such a state of penury that they were threatened by creditors.

Moina also experienced some strange events during her work on the project. She was responsible for the design on the frontispiece of the translation and insisted that parts of her design were altered 'by no mortal hand'. At this stage Moina was anxious to establish herself once more as an artist, and perhaps provide some income to swell the Mathers coffers. Her plans did not bear fruit as her efforts were far too idiosyncratic to have any popular appeal. She had also embraced her husband's intransigence and was not prepared to change her style to suit the market.

Mathers must have been aware that by engaging in the intense concentration required to translate the work he was at risk of being 'taken over' by the magical influences contained therein. Mathers' character was never one of detachment, exactly the reverse; his ability to totally involve himself in his thoughts was both a virtue and a debilitating weakness. Dion Fortune, in her many writings upon the nature of magic and its application offers this plea for sobriety:

It is very necessary to the health and stability...to keep the planes of consciousness strictly separated, and this is one of the first things he learns to do when taught the technique of the Mysteries.[57]

Even closer to home was the text of Moina Mathers' lecture delivered in 1893. It includes this pertinent advice:

'...we should *not* retire from the world, for we can succeed in perfecting ourselves in what is required of us without isolation.'

She goes on to suggest that,

...isolation tends to make a man egotistical...this Egotism...will yet be a far greater snare to him, as being more subtle and therefore less easy to be perceived and checked.[58]

We can be sure that Moina was not in the habit of offering such homilies to her husband. However, had she done so, and Mathers heeded her words, things might have turned out very differently indeed.

Mathers soon began to grow anxious over the Order. He was convinced that his authority in England was slipping away. He had come to believe that unless he had sole authority in the Golden Dawn, any occult business would not be conducted correctly. In the manner of every tyrant since civilization began, he decided to permanently remove the opposition. Mathers appeared to focus on Westcott as the obstacle to his obtaining exclusive leadership of the Golden Dawn, and determined he would be the first to go. Deposing Westcott would not be easy, the task posed practical problems, as we shall see.

In the meantime, Mathers attempted to maintain control of the English Order by appointing four officers whose duty it was to report directly to him. In so doing, he sought to ensure that his wishes alone were carried out, rather than any directive made by Westcott. He chose his cohorts carefully – Annie Horniman, Florence Farr, Percy Bullock and Dr. Edward Berridge.

Bullock and Berridge are names unfamiliar in our tale so far. Who were they? Percy Bullock was a clerk with Slaughter and May, a well-known firm of solicitors. He joined the Isis-Urania Temple in 1890, adopting *Levavi Oculos* ('I will lift up mine eyes') as his motto. He became Sub-Imperator in 1896, the successor to Dr. Berridge. This gentleman, who joined the ranks soon after the Order was formed, had the motto *Resurgam* ('I shall rise again'). The quartet of Horniman, Farr, Bullock and Berridge comprised by far the most influential members of the Order, and at this stage they were prepared to unquestioningly accept Mathers' authority.

In 1895, after receiving a further legacy, Horniman had firmly established herself in the highest echelons of the rich in England. She had leased an apartment in Montague Mansions in Portman

Square, one of the most select districts of London. Horniman particularly relished being given extra responsibilities in the Order. When Mathers gave her, as she saw it, a higher rank she took her new duties very seriously indeed. Ironically, it was to be this zeal that precipitated the first crisis in the Order.

While in Paris, Mather's obsession with his military connections increased. We are indebted to Yeats for his impression of Mathers at this time.

> At night he would dress himself in Highland dress, and dance the sword dance, and his mind brooded upon the ramifications of clans and tartans. Yet I have at moments doubted whether he had seen the Highlands, or even...Scotland itself.[59]

His delusions became more grandiose as the days passed. A particularly nationalistic period of Scottish history – the times of Bonny Prince Charlie and the 1745 Rebellion – became an obsession with Mathers. He would expound in great length upon the Jacobite cause to anyone who would listen. He cast himself in heroic roles with his delusions assuming almighty proportions. According to Yeats, Mathers,

> ...imagined a Napoleonic role for himself, a Europe transformed according to his fancy, Egypt restored, a Highland Principality, and even offered subordinate posts to unlikely people.[60]

Mathers attempted to combine the qualities of the warrior and the magician, an ambition that has an ancient heritage, particularly amongst shamans. Carlos Castaneda proposes this as one of the themes in Don Juan's magical philosophy. The wizard constantly tests the courage and resources of his magical pupil. Joseph Campbell also describes the training necessary for the heavenly champion.

Sicut incoelo et in terra: the initiated warrior is an agent of the divine will; his training is not only in manual but also in spiritual skills. Magic (the supernatural power of the thunderbolt), as well as physical force and chemical poison gibes the lethal energy to his blows. A consummate master would require no physical weapon at all; the power of his magic would suffice.[61]

Mathers certainly possessed a strong will, but other qualities in his personality made it difficult for him to effectively fulfil the role of the warrior/magician. His astrological chart provides some clues. He has Aries in the ascendant, Mars in Trine with the Sun, Moon and Uranus, and Mars is in opposition to Neptune. This gave him a martial streak and a forceful will, but one that was unbalanced. It was an aspect that made him overbearing. Mars' opposition to Neptune, the planet of illusions, gave rise to his misplaced messianic tendencies.

Yeats described him as, 'courageous in thought and kind in act'[62] but did not deny that he demonstrated behaviour akin to megalomania. The poet commented on these conflicting aspects of Mathers in his recollections.

Once when I met him in the street in his Highland clothes, with several knives in his stocking, he said, 'When I am dressed like this I feel like a walking flame'...everything he did was but an attempt to feel like a walking flame. Yet at heart he was...gentle, and perhaps even a little timid.[63]

Yeats concluded that Mathers' difficulty in reconciling the conflicting aspects of his nature put him under great strain. One sincerely hopes that his occult studies brought him some relief; they certainly continued to occupy his time in Paris. He undoubtedly found some solace in the company of Moina; her passive aggression always acquiesced to her husband's will. She supported him in whatever decision he made, however arbitrary or mistaken.

Not long after establishing the Paris Temple, Mathers' attention became intensely focused on the magical traditions of Egypt. He and Moina had now become, in their own minds at least, the personification of Isis and Osiris. Mathers was acutely aware of the symbolism of resurrection. He considered that experiencing a continual rebirth was an essential occult practice and enhanced the progress of the magician. Osiris epitomises a principle of magic, one that demands complete sacrifice of the self in order to gain access to divine power. Perhaps Mathers also yearned to embrace the martial aspect of Mentu the Egyptian war god, a personification of the scorching power of Ra the sun god.

Mathers' involvement with Osiris and all Egyptian magic was no pose. He was also much taken with Ptah, who brought the gift of life to the world. This deity dreamed creation in his heart, and then called the world into being. As Florence Farr proposed in her own writings, '...The priests gained power by the identification of themselves with the types of natural forces, known to us as gods.'[64] Regrettably, Mathers' adopting of any archetypes only increased his tendency to become bombastic. In his hands the archetype soon became a stereotype.

Moina, being born under the mutable sign of Pisces personified the watery element. She fully identified with Isis. Isis is the lunar deity *in excelsis* and the ebbing and flowing of the tides are under her dominion. The cult of Isis is the epitome of the worship of the feminine. Isis is the most powerful and the most highly regarded of any goddess – 'Goddess of Heaven, Goddess of Earth, and Goddess of the Underworld.' The Roman writer Apuleius in *The Golden Ass* reports her words,

I am nature, the universal Mother, mistress of all the elements, primordial child of time, sovereign of all things spiritual, queen of the dead, queen also of the immortals, the single manifestation of all gods that are...Some know me as Juno, some as Bellona...The Egyptians who excel in ancient learning call me by my true name...Queen Isis.[65]

Mathers saw the spiritual roles of male and female as being equal. He recognized that the polarity between Priest and Priestess results in a much greater magic than the practitioner who works alone. It is to Mathers' credit that he supported women as practitioners of magic in their own right. To any who questioned this, Mathers had a swift rejoinder, 'The numerous advanced female occult students of the present day are the best answer to this.'[66] He protested of,

...the usual injustice to and jealousy of women which has distinguished men for so many ages, and which as far as I can see arises purely and simply from an innate consciousness that were women once admitted to compete with them on any plane without being handicapped as they have been for so many centuries, the former would speedily prove their superiority...[67]

Mathers had given the title 'Isis Movement' to his own preoccupations with the mysteries of Ancient Egypt. With Moina, he had rehearsed 'The Rite of Isis', a theatrical performance that dramatically depicted their devotions. A journalist, Jules Bois, persuaded them to give a public performance of 'The Rite' at the Bodiniere Theatre in March of 1899. The response was mixed. Some of the audience were openly appreciative, while some of the press reports that appeared later had a comical tone. Whatever the reception, it did not deter the Mathers from giving two further performances, but in a more private setting. It was Moina's contribution that ensured the success of the Rite.

In the autumn of 1900, the Mathers moved to Montmartre.

Their involvement with the Isis ritual did not lessen. With the assistance of a sponsor they were able to put on an even grander spectacle which received a complimentary review in a French magazine. The journalist Andre Gaucher described its *piece de resistance*.

> The enormous statue was in fact the Egyptian god, [Osiris]...Even in Egypt the existence of such a monumental granite statue would have been extraordinary, but in Paris it was totally incomprehensible. From the top of the statue a luminous phosphorescent beam circled the hall, inexplicably bathing the worshippers in the changing light.[68]

Despite their growing reputation, a regular income from magical activities or any other source still proved elusive. In November, 1900, Mathers was trying to touch Westcott, of all the people he could have chosen, for a loan of ten pounds.

VI

Dawn of Western Magic

Think of a place and thou art there already.
Axiom of Hermetic Magic

To fully appreciate what was involved in the doings of the Golden Dawn, it is important to understand some basic concepts about magic. The word 'magic' derives from the Greek *magikos*. An even older root is from the Persian *magus* or *magi*. This is the title that was bestowed upon the ancient priestly caste and celebrated in the Biblical tale of the 'Wise Men from the East'.

The Oxford English Dictionary gives as a definition of magic, 'the art of influencing events, control of nature'. The word is sometimes written as *magick* so as to differentiate the practice from *conjuring* or *legerdemain* (slight of hand). Aleister Crowley always wrote the word in this manner, partly because he considered that 'K', being the eleventh letter of the alphabet, this had great occult significance. Eleven is regarded as a 'master' number by numerologists.

In the West, our ancestors devoted much time in attempting to understand their environment, and perhaps the human predicament, though they would scarcely have regarded life in such terms. Employing magic was the way they dealt with any idea of the 'unknown'. The discovery of the solar and lunar cycles and the procession of the seasons gave rise to celebrations and evocations to mark such events. They approached the universe in awe of its wonders and eventually it began to share its secrets with them.

A community's magician, or *shaman* as he might be called, worked from the premise that, 'if we do *this* in *that* order, we will have a clearer idea of the nature of the divine.' It is neatly summarized in the old magical adage – 'as above so below'. The successful magician eventually attains a state where the two spheres are interchangeable – the seen reflects the unseen.

The most workable definition of magic comes from Dion Fortune – 'The ability to control natural forces at will'. The magician attempts to *utilize* these natural forces, in contrast to the mystic who attempts to become one with them. Let us examine the energies particular to the Magician. We can best do this by studying the card of the Ryder Waite Tarot entitled 'The Magician'.

The figure stands before his magical table – his altar – on which are his tools, representing the earth elements he has learned to control: the cup (water), the sword (air) and the pentacle (earth). He holds a wand, which represents the element of fire, or action aloft in his right hand. The divine power he has invoked through the wand flows from the heavens above to the Earth below.

The magician occupies a sacred space between the blooms of flowers in the heaven and those on earth. He has manifested the blooms of earth through a magical process using his magical imagination. He has created a thought form of the flowers which he ensouls with the divine energy he has invoked. He then channels these energies through the passive fingers of his left hand pointing towards the earth. The power that he personifies flows around the lemniscate (the symbol of infinity) above his head. His slight smile implies that he knows only too well the role he plays in creation – he is a channel, rather than the source of the divine energies.

The 'imagination' the magician employs is more profound than the sort that we experience in our normal daily consciousness. It is not the realm of daydreams – something divorced from the meaningful. George Russell provides these comments, which constitute an excellent, if some what prolix definition of the magical imagination. For him it is,

...a higher thing than vision, and a much rarer thing, for in the act of imagination that which is hidden in being...is named manifest and a transfiguration takes place like that we imagine in the Spirit when it willed 'let there be light'. Imagination is not a vision of something which already exists...but by imagination what exists in latency or essence is out-realised and is given a form in thought, and we can contemplate with full consciousness that which hitherto has been unrevealed, or only intuitionally surmised. In imagination there is revelation of the self to the self, and some definite change in being...Here images appear in consciousness...endow(ed)...with life, motion and voice.[69]

The process of Magical manifestation begins with a shift in consciousness. The magical practitioner moves from this world into another, taking a step 'beyond the veil'. The High Priestess card of the Tarot is a splendid depiction of this experience. Looking particularly knowing, the priestess sits before the veil. It represents simultaneously a desire for knowledge, and the place where it may be found – the otherworld. What can be seen beyond the curtain is an endless stretch of water. This appears to be calm, yet beneath the surface powerful and mysterious currents are always on the move. The key to every puzzle is to be found beyond the veil, a place of fascination and delight.

Occultists in the West have always experimented with the forces of the universe on both a microcosmic and macrocosmic level. If the practitioner can activate an event on one level, it will be reflected in another. The material that makes up the physical form, however, is owned by none, except by The Goddess. Every atom in our bodies has seen service in another form, at another time. All is in a state of constant change and this must be so, for change is energy. As the universe is composed of atoms, and man is part of the universe, the two are indivisible. Man reflects the universe so, *ipso facto*, man is the universe. That belief is at the centre of Western magic, and it is what enables the practitioner to alter the fabric of reality.

The forces that the magician needs in order practice magic are always available for his use. He has only to tune in to them and he may manifest anything that he desires, although his efforts may require perseverance. The only proviso for success is that his efforts must be at one with the Divine Will. Without this, no amount of effort will bring success.

The philosophy and practices of The Golden Dawn followed the 'Western Magical Tradition' and in fact, came to further develop and define this tradition. The term is used to delineate a particular school of occult practice, distinct from those based on Oriental principles. The Oriental willingness to accept fate as the arbiter of all things temporal has never been accepted in the West. The inhabitants of this part of the globe have always had a desire to find out about the nature of existence in order to alter their lives.

The Western Magical Tradition has roots which include the systems of thought from Greece, Chaldea, Egypt, Celtic and Norse mythology, Arthurian lore and the Qabalah. What these traditions have in common is the desire and belief that the magician has the power to control natural forces. What follows is a brief explication of the different strands which make up the bedrock of the Golden Dawn philosophy.

It can be speculated that the very origins of the Western Magical Tradition spring from the area once known as Mesopotamia. Within this area was Sumer – 'The Land of the Lords of Brightness'. Ancient Egypt was the only other civilization considered to be more advanced than the Sumerians. By 2,300 B.C. they had invented the wheel and the first system of writing – known as syllabaric. They also pioneered various social systems including government, schools and courts. Instrumental in the discovery of astronomy, they used this knowledge to develop a calendar based on lunar changes. Their extensive efforts at agriculture involved vast feats of engineering to provide irrigation for crops. Temples which incorporated music and dance in their devotions were an essential aspect of their lives. It is from this pragmatic, visionary and masterful culture that the philosophy and science of magic comes. Nearly four millennia later, this ancient civilization held up a mirror to the Golden Dawn and its adherents.

The Egyptian tradition was also held in very high esteem by Mathers. It became an important part of the teachings and rituals of the Golden Dawn. Mathers felt Osiris was a particularly powerful god and often took his form in rituals. Osiris is the son of Geb – the Earth – and Nut – the sky. He has much potency on the earthly plane. He is seen as the archetypal vegetation god by some Egyptologists and at times he is depicted as green in colour, reflecting fertility and growth. Osiris has the title 'King of the Living'. Egyptian priests considered the 'blessed dead' to be 'The Living Ones'. Osiris is also given the titles 'Lord of Love' and 'Lord of Silence'. He is renowned for his mercy, and grants eternal life to the kings of Egypt through his powers.

In later traditions Osiris is Adonis, Mithras, and the Fisher King of the Arthurian legends. With Osiris, both The Ram and Khnum the ram-headed god of Egypt are linked to the Spring. Astrologically this is the time of Aries the Ram, symbolised by the seed and new growth.

Water, and more specifically its denizen the fish, is a major part of the Osiris legend. Osiris is dismembered by Set and then physically restored by Isis with the help of Thoth. One part of him is missing – rather an important item; his member has been eaten by a fish. Isis uses her magic to fashion a replacement from clay, and Osiris' manhood is restored. The trials of Osiris are seen as the price to pay for gaining wisdom. The gods, impressed by the stoicism of Osiris and the devotion of Isis, bestow their rewards upon them. Osiris is made god of the underworld, Isis is the Queen of Heaven who sitteth among the stars. The link with

Christ as a sacrificial deity is hard to overlook. In the words of Wallis Budge, the renowned Egyptologist,

...because he (Osiris) had conquered death the righteous also might conquer death...in Osiris (is) the prototype of Christ, and in the pictures of and statues of Isis suckling her son Horus...the prototypes of the Virgin Mary and her child.[70]

The god Horus, the child of Isis, was also held in high esteem, the *Wadjet* or Eye of Horus being a very powerful sign of protection. The symbol was placed above the entrance to the Vault of the Golden Dawn where members entered for initiation in the esteemed Second Order.

In the Egyptian pantheon there are several female deities. Hathor is the Mirror of Isis; Maat, who wears a feather in her headdress, is the Goddess of Justice, Truth and Mercy. She is considered to have made order from the primeval chaos. Sekhmet, depicted with a woman's body and a lion's head, is the daughter of Ra. She has the title 'the avenger of wrongs'.

Isis is the goddess who epitomizes all that is feminine. Initially, both men and women served as priests and priestesses in the Temples of Isis. In a later era this was to change and those who served Isis were exclusively women. They were midwives, healers and interpreters of dreams. It was said that these wonderful creatures could control the weather by braiding or combing their hair. This talent may explain the belief of the ancient Egyptians that all knots had magical power. The knot in the cord that fastens the priest's robe reflects this belief.

Isis (together with Thoth), is a deity much associated with the occult. She declares, 'I am Isis the goddess, the possessor of magic, who performs magic, effective of speech, excellent of words.' The relationship between Thoth and Isis, personified as the Magician and the High Priestess, is most significant. The wisdom of Isis is reflected in the magus – it is the divine spark in man. Isis, as the moon, is the Hidden Wisdom. The Magician, as mercury, is the Lord of Wisdom. Venus, as the Earth or *form of nature*, responds to the magic of both.

Thoth is the god of magic and also writing, variously titled 'The Lord of the Divine Books' and 'Scribe of the Company of the Gods'. He is also the 'Voice of Ra' who evokes the spark of Creation. The ability to command spirits, and make the universe obey the wishes of the magician, depends much upon his use of words. With his voice Thoth sets all in motion – the world begins to turn. In magic, words work in tandem with magical gestures.

The forces of the natural world do not respond to reason, but powers beyond the rational. The words chosen, and the manner in which they are delivered are the keys to any effective ceremony. As the god of writing, Thoth created the Egyptian system of hieroglyphs. The pictograms were a collection of sacred symbols. Thus, to the ordinary man writing was a mystical art, a reflection of the divine. It is all too easy, living in an era of information overload as we do, to regard words as trivial things. The Ancient Egyptians entertained no such view, and Thoth, in his unlimited power of manifestation through communication, reflects this approach.

Devotion to the deities was paramount in the whole of Egyptian society. When supplications were offered to heaven, the faith of the devotee was unshakeable. Those who prayed believed that they became the gods themselves. This is a fundamental principle of ritual magic, one embraced by Dion Fortune, though without the obvious 'prayer' aspect. The practioner subsequently becoming as a god or goddess is the goal of invoking any particular deity.

Mathers had an interesting perspective on the common Egyptian depiction of a god or a goddess as a human figure with the head of an animal or bird.

...animals and human beings possess similar emotions; ...all beings living on the earth experience one and the same divine life; ...the Unfathomable appears behind various earthly masks and ... the eternal feelings of the universe are summed up not only in the form of a human being but also in those of the animals.[71]

The school of magic practiced in the Egyptian system subsequently became the tradition of 'Hermetic', receiving its name from the Greek god Hermes. In the Egyptian pantheon he was Thoth, for the Romans – Mercury. Naomi Ozaniec explains Hermeticism in terms of the Sephiroth Hod.

The Virtue of Hod is Truthfulness. This is not only a personal virtue but a fundamental belief that the truth of nature, ultimate reality, can be discerned through the powers given to the human being. The Hermetic view was an empowering one which authorized the individual spiritual quest. This is a stream of wisdom that never fails. It is the Ageless Wisdom, the Perennial Philosophy, and the Natural Philosophy. Like a magnet it calls out to the questioning mind, the restless spirit and the yearning soul.[72]

The roots of hermetic philosophy reach far into the past. The Great Library at Alexandria was sacked by Julius Caesar in 48 B.C. It suffered various later attacks culminating in its total destruction by the Muslims in A.D. 642. The whole of 'Hermetic Magic' is based on two works rescued from the flames – the *Corpus Hermeticum* and the *Emerald Tablet of Hermes Trismegistus*. This 'Wisdom of the Whole Universe' as it modestly claims to be, consists of a treatise on alchemy, astrology and theurgy. These components of Hermeticism were important aspects of the Western esoteric tradition.

Alchemy is often mistakenly regarded as solely an attempt to change base metal into gold. This is to drastically misunderstand the premise of the operations conducted by a true alchemist. The goal – the *Magnum Opus* – is that of achieving perfection. In alchemy, birth, death and resurrection are the basis for metaphysical as well as chemical investigation.

Astrology is regarded as a metaphorical system beyond the laws of physics. The planets are seen as symbols that may have an enduring influence upon our actions. The degree in which they affect us is within our powers to decide.

Theurgy (the root of the word is from *Theo* – god + *ergos* – working) is concerned with the two types of magic. *Goetia* is an alliance with demons to fulfil the magician's purposes, while Theurgy depends for its success upon an affinity with angels. The ultimate intention of both alchemy and theurgy is to be united with the Divine Consciousness.

Hermeticism runs in parallel with the Neo-Platonic school of philosophy, espousing the theory of reincarnation. Through their Masonic and Rosicrucian background, Mathers and Westcott would have regarded theurgy – divine working – as being wholly part of the 'universal mind'. Neo-Platonists espoused this philosophy from A.D. 200 onwards. Within it, the One is capable of emanating the Divine Mind- *Nous* – and also the World Soul – *Psyche*. To the Neo-Platonist, the purpose of magic was for man to reunite with the demiurge. This deification implies a merging with the One in a process called *Henosis*.

Rosicrucianism embraces both Hermetic and Christian principles. Its symbol is a combination of the Rose and the Cross – the soul attached irrevocably to the Four Elements. A philosophical system originating in the late Middle Ages, it flowered at a time of great religious upheaval in Europe and was eagerly embraced by many. Its association with Elizabethan figures in England, such as Francis Bacon and John Dee, gave it the reputation of being part of the new Renaissance thought.

It is to be remembered that with the Renaissance came a new

spirit of tolerance towards the study of metaphysics. Before this time any individual discovered to be involved with alchemy or magic in any form ran the risk of being summarily condemned to imprisonment, or even death. Even possessing a book on magic was highly dangerous. The owner of a grimoire could be accused of 'diabolism' and persecuted as a heretic by the Church. Thus, magic was forced underground and its reputation, and even its *raison d'être*, was lost in an ever thickening fog.

The Qabalah is an ancient Judaic spiritual tradition that was discovered and later embraced by the Rosicrucians. The Qabalah is defined by Hebrew scholars as a system of philosophy that seeks to understand the nature of God. *Qabalah*[73] means 'to receive'. These teachings consist of mystical visions and interpretations of traditional Jewish texts which were conveyed orally from teacher to student. As it existed solely as an oral tradition, written texts were much limited. One key Qabalistic text is the *Zohar* – the 'book of splendour' which was first discovered in the thirteenth century. Included in its teachings is the complex glyph of the *Tree of Life* which represents the process of creation. These teaching were carefully guarded and were shared only with men over forty, who displayed maturity and wisdom. It was felt that the teachings were dangerous for any others, and they might become mad, or even die, by using them injudiciously.

From its inception, nearly two millennia passed before occultist Cornelius Agrippa, and later Eliphas Levi, promoted the Qabalah as a magical system. Levi realized that within the Tree of Life lay a school of philosophy appropriate to the consciousness of the West. The Medieval Qabalah embraced the notion that each of the Ten Sephiroth was emanations of the Godhead. This is not a polytheistic system; the Sephiroth are not separate gods, but successive points in a continual decent of divine energy toward manifestation on earth. They represent different aspects of the Godhead.

The Sephiroth are aligned in three pillars, a masculine pillar of mercy, a feminine pillar of severity and a middle pillar of equilibrium. Energy descends in the pattern of a lightning flashing from the Godhead; it repeatedly criss-crosses from the right, (masculine) side of the tree to the left, (feminine) side and then descends toward the middle pillar where polarities are resolved. There are points of balance and unity symbolised in the Tree of Life without which manifestation cannot occur. The technique of achieving these ends was part of the Golden Dawn teachings.

Enochian Magic was also a development which was to become an important part of Western Magic. The birth of Enochian philosophy came with the investigations of Dr. John Dee and Edward Kelley, the renowned Elizabethan occultists. Much of their knowledge was gained from the scrying carried out by Kelley. He contacted three classes of heavenly beings: angels, archangels and fallen angels. Kelley developed a working method for his magical system by taking the ethereal communications he received and combining them with another source. This was the philosophy contained within 'apocryphal documents', namely writings dating from the third or fourth centuries B.C. ascribed to the great-grandfather of Noah. All this made up the 'Book of Enoch'. The most useful part of the work for Dee and Kelley's purposes was 'The Book of the Watchers'. This details not only an astronomical plan but also the Four Watchtowers, the Great Quadrangles and the Tablet of Union. There are nineteen Enochian Keys, or Calls, which were used as magical evocations.

Hermeticism avowed that the transition of Man from the pure Soul to an entity enslaved by the Earth was the tragedy of the human condition. In Homer's *Hymn to Ceres*, Persephone recalls her own fall:

'...the pleasant flowers...with joy I was plucking them, when the earth yawned beneath, and out leaped the strong King, the Many-Receiver, and went bearing me, deeply sorrowing under the earth in his golden chariot, and I cried aloud.'[74]

Thus it was the goal of hermetic magic to help man regain his divinity. By the Age of Enlightenment, the antipathy towards the occult had ebbed and popular opinion had almost drifted into a general indifference. With the birth of scientific thought any idea of 'the mysteries' was regarded as merely archaic superstition. The turning point for magic in the West came in the nineteenth century, its saviour a stout Parisian – Eliphas Levi.

Born Alphonse Louis Constant, the child of devout French Catholics, Levi became the most significant figure in the occult world since the European magi of the seventeenth century. This extraordinary man almost single-handedly created what came to be the Western Magical Tradition. His influence upon the Golden Dawn was inestimable. Encountering witchcraft in his youth, Levi went on to become interested in all things esoteric. In 1861, he was made a Master Mason, and in the same year met Kenneth Mackenzie.

The role of that singular gentleman in the beginnings of the Golden Dawn has already been noted. Levi journeyed to England and met Bulwer-Lytton, the First Baron Knebworth, a celebrated occult writer. The contribution of Lytton to the path of nineteenth century magic should not be underestimated. His novel *Zanoni*, with its theme of a secret order of extra-terrestrial beings who protect and guide the world, has a hint of the Masters of Blavatsky and the Secret Chiefs of the Golden Dawn.

Lytton encouraged Levi with the writing of his two great magical treatises *Transcendental magic its Doctrine and Ritual* (1885) and *The Key to the Great Mysteries* (1861). A later meeting with the baron in the company of Count Alexander Branicki, a Polish exile, prompted Levi to begin a study of alchemy. Through the offices of Alexander Dumas, the son of the celebrated writer, Levi was later elected to the Society of Paris, a consortium of thinkers and intellectuals. He was thus able to maintain a reasonable living in his middle years.

Levi is justly remembered for his two magical treatises.

Within their pages, an account of a ritual to raise the spirit of Apollonius of Tyana, a renowned magician of antiquity, makes most extraordinary reading. Levi succeeded in the operation, but concluded that the exercise was 'an actual drunkenness of the imagination'. The experience convinced him that this was 'sufficient to establish the real efficacy of magical ceremonies.'[75] Levi, laudably, advised 'the greatest caution to those who propose devoting themselves to similar experiences'. If Levi, a disciplined and knowledgeable practitioner, was moved to issue such a warning then we may conclude that evocation is a practice not recommended to the amateur. Let those who would be tempted to 'dabble' take heed.

In his treatises Levi expresses quite complex ideas in simple terms. He does not propose that the magical path is anything other than a hard one, and offers only the promise that magical knowledge may lead to the ultimate perception. He unequivocally states that, '...magic implies superiority, mastership (and) majority, and majority signifies emancipation by knowledge.'

The magician, he continues, 'endures oblivion willingly because he is lord of his own happiness, and expects or fears nothing from the caprice of fortune.' The attainment of a personal equilibrium is gauged to be of more worth than happiness. 'He possesses that which he seeks, namely, profound peace.' The magus distances himself from any conventional morality secure in that, 'His hope is certitude, for he knows that god is eternal and evil transitory.' Levi identifies three fundamental principles of magic: firstly that the material plane is only one of many states of consciousness; secondly, that the human will may achieve anything; and thirdly, that a change in the microcosm affects the macrocosm.

Other fields of knowledge developed in the nineteenth and twentieth century that were to become important strands in the Western Magical Tradition. It cannot be mere coincidence that the researches into the unconscious made by Freud, and later Jung, were made public at the same time as a growing interest of all things magical. An awareness that states of perception beyond the ordinary existed slowly began to be accepted. The term 'parallel universe' was not in general usage though it was to be so later in the C20[th]. mainly through the work of Hugh Everett and others adapting the original theses of Einstein and Bohr. Research into cosmology, neurology, and quantum physics, began to suggest that the mind was the source of all that we perceive.

Finally, the contribution of myth to Western Magic cannot be ignored. The wisdom of the fabled land of Atlantis was preserved in druidic lore and the wizardry of Merlin. There are elements of Atlantis in the kingdom of Avalon, wherein lies the Grail. King Arthur and the Knights of the Round Table embark upon their eternal Quest, in the same way that the magus searches for truth beyond the veil. The Norse myths typified the milieu of kings, queens and heroes who in turn reflected the harsh reality of their setting. We now begin to see how the Western way is an active tradition, one that combines the nobility of the warrior with the nearby world of fairies and spirits. All of this, combined with systems of philosophy such as the Qabalah and the Tarot, helped to produce the new magic, a system embraced by the Golden Dawn.

VII

The Magic of the Golden Dawn

Some tradition has been preserved by societies of wise men, who, because of the persecutions...concealed themselves and whispered the old teaching one to another.
Aleister Crowley

Further to the debate in the previous chapter, it is interesting to speculate as to why the Golden Dawn championed the Western Magical tradition. Perhaps occultists of the day had an unconscious reaction to the doctrine of the Theosophical Society. Blavatsky in her writings made it plain that she did not look kindly upon spiritual traditions other than Buddhism. To redress the balance, the time had come for those in the West to rediscover the great magical heritage they had almost forgotten. The realization brought a new exuberance to Western occultism. The founding members of the Golden Dawn had a background in Freemasonry, Rosicrucianism, Enochian magic and the Qabalah. Mather's fascination with the system of Egyptian magic was to steer the Order in this direction, although not all members were inclined to accept this as we shall see.

Mary Anne Atwood's *A Suggestive Inquiry into Hermetic Philosophy and Alchemy* is the basis of all Hermetic studies within the Golden Dawn. Published in 1850, its philosophy was particularly attractive to Waite, as it promotes the idea of a divine entity that determines all. Waite was undeniably a Monotheist, and it was probably for this reason he chose to shun Mathers' involvement with the Egyptian deities. Both Waite and Westcott wrote about Hermetic magic, the former being particularly prolific on the subject.

It is small wonder that Waite, in homage to his beliefs, ensured that the name chosen for the reformed Order in 1902 would be the *Hermetic Society of the M.R.* ('M.R.' is *Morgenrothe* – 'Golden Dawn' in German). He was not directly involved in its leadership that honour was given to Brodie-Innes, Felkin and Bullock. It is quite likely that being responsible for the title of the order meant more to him than having authority within it. More significantly for Waite and his followers, the later order was espousing a universal religion that encompasses all faiths. The lifelong mission of Madame Blavatsky was to bring about such a spiritual unification. This end is still of primary importance in the principles of Theosophy.

The approach to the Qabalah adopted by The Golden Dawn was predominantly that espoused by Mathers. Mathers had studied Levi's work and clearly agreed that the Qabalah was a valuable magical tool. In addition to the value placed on it by Levi, the likelihood of the Qabalah originating in Egypt may have made this system attractive to Mathers. A well-know Egyptologist, E. Wallace Budge felt that it was likely that Moses had learned the power of magic during his sojourn in Egypt.[76] As Moses is credited with receiving the mystical teachings of the Qabalah, could these powers have been part of these teachings? Mathers may have felt there was a connection, as these comments by Budge suggest.

> The historian Mas'udi mentions an instance of the powers of working magic possessed by a certain Jew, which proves that the magical practices of the Egyptians had passed eastwards and had found a congenial home among the Jews who lived in and about Babylon...he raised up several apparitions, and made a king of huge stature, who was mounted upon a horse, gallop about in the desert...He then transformed himself into a camel and walked upon a rope...[77]

Mathers' own published study of the Qabalah, *Kabbalah Unveiled*, is a dense document propounding his own understanding of the Zohar. In the Qabalah, the Sephira Tiphareth embodies divine sacrifice. Mathers may have particularly identified with this Sephira upon the Tree of Life which is associated with sacrifice. He possessed a certain messianic complex, and continually asserted that he sacrificed himself at the altar of duty.

These traditions were woven into the structure and instruction for the students of the Golden Dawn. In magic, motive is all, and it should be performed only with one motive in mind – to bring light into the world. Laudably, this was the intent of the Golden Dawn. In Israel Regardie's words,

> ...the whole system had as its objective the bringing down of the Light. For it is by that Light that the golden banner of the inner life may be exalted; it is in Light where lies healing and the power of growth.[78]

From the very beginning this principle was instilled in all initiates. The Neophyte was adjured with these words by the Hierophant, 'Child of Earth, long hast thou dwelt in darkness. Quit the night and seek the day.' It is difficult to improve on the ethos that the Order promoted, namely that through study, discipline and the highest ethical standards, knowledge may be obtained. It was also implied that joining the ranks of a magical fraternity was a high honour and not one to be taken lightly.

Above all, it was important for the fledgling magician to respond to the command 'know thyself'. He or she was expected to have an understanding of his place in the universe and of the role they played in the process of magical creation. Every aspect of our mortal existence can never be anything but a Hall of Mirrors. Even the power of manifestation, the goal of any magical ritual, must eventually be regarded as yet another illusion. If this is not taken into account, there is a danger that the magician will become inflated with an idea of his own importance in the great scheme of things. This is a mistake often made by the beginner in magic and one that always leads to the path being lost. It may be regained but only with the most courageous efforts.

The ambitious soul seeks initiation, yet even once it has been gained it only temporarily at rest. The young magician needs to overcome this restlessness so that he might develop the centeredness needed by a great magus. As Dion Fortune tells us,

> The initiate of the Greater Mysteries is known by his serenity and impersonal attitude in all the relations of life. He knows how to be still and let the powers he has set in motion carry out the work.[79]

One method for developing this balance was for every adept to study the Tree of Life, and to learn to balance their energies using a meditation based on the Middle Pillar of the Tree.[80] Through this practice, the neophyte learned to put aside notions of duality – good and evil, superior and inferior, even male and female. As we must realize, Heaven and Hell were inventions of man, not the Cosmos. As Heraclitus declared, 'To God all things are fair and good and right, but men hold some things wrong and some right.'[81]

The way that the Order offered instruction was in accord with the ancient notion of magic being a means of sharing occult and esoteric knowledge. The term 'occult' means 'hidden', 'esoteric' – 'for the few'. Should all have access to the mysteries? Perhaps more pertinently, should everyone be allowed to practice magic? The Golden Dawn did not consider they should, hence its system of grades. The respect given to the 'Tree of Life' was reflected in the fact that each grade in the Order was assigned to a particular Sephira. The Structure of the Grades was based upon the Rosicrucian model. There were three Orders, with five grades within the first order and three grades within the second:

First Order
Neophyte 0=0
Zelator 1=10
Theoricus 2=9
Practicus 3=8
Philosophus 4=7 (Portal)

Second Order
Adeptus Minor 5=6
Adeptus Major 6=5
Adeptus Exemptus 7=4

Third Order
Magister Templi 8=3
Magus 9=2
Ipsissimus 10=1

Apart from the Neophyte, the paired numbers relate to the positions on the Tree of Life. The first number is the number of steps up from *Malkuth,* at the bottom of the tree, the second the amount down from *Kether,* at the top of the tree. The First Order Grades related to the four elements. Moving from one grade to another was dependent upon passing an oral and a written examination. Admission to the Second Order was also dependent upon the consent of the adepts of that order. It was possible to take examinations to enable an Adept to gain a higher rank within this Second Order and access to the libraries of the lodges was always available. These held the most impressive works on magic that then existed in the West. Sumptuous collections of the most priceless magical artefacts were held by the Order, in greater numbers than those held in private hands.

The emphasis on the examinations that enabled the candidate to pass to the Second Order was paramount. Gaining this meant that the practice of magic could then actually begin. The subjects studied were symbolism (Astrological and Alchemical), the Qabalah, the Tarot and Geomancy. On entry to the Second Order they prepared for participation in ritual by making talismans and magical weapons. The only 'ritual' divulged to First Order initiates was the 'Banishing Ritual of the Pentagram', as it is generally known. Nowadays, this can be found on numerous websites on the Internet. In 1888, its procedures would have been only known to a select few.

Initiates learned to embark upon an astral journey in a series of stages. Neophytes developed 'ordinary' clairvoyance by employing paraphernalia such as a crystal ball, or the traditional method of scrying – using a dish filled with black ink. The intention was to encourage the initiate to open their inner vision and achieve genuine 'seeing' – hence the term 'seer'. The next stage was to develop the ability to journey on the astral plane. This technique was described as 'projecting'. Entering into another world, and engaging with whatever was to be discovered there was the real goal.

There were several methods used by the Order, these included meditations on the paths of the Tree of Life, the Major Arcana of the Tarot, or the Tattwas (explained below). In addition to the ten Sephiroth on the Tree of Life, the twenty-two paths between them were often the focus of meditations. These are rich in associations – astrological symbols, a Hebrew letter, a Tarot – all are assigned to each path. Annie Horniman was familiar with the use of Major Arcana cards for meditation, and specifically taught her students to use the High Priestess card in this way. The method is set out with the pragmatic air of the true practitioner, as this passage demonstrates:

I take the High Priestess the Moon in my hand and look at the figure and imagine it as a stately woman in golden mitre in red gold-bordered robes on a throne with a book in her hand. I make the Lunar Hexagram saying Shaddai El Chai, Gabriel,

Malka, Chasmodai, Gimel and pass through the figure I have made, as we do through a Tattva symbol.[82]

The Tattwas (or Tattvas) are archetypal symbols. Originating in the East, they have been employed in meditation for many centuries. There are five symbols – the four elements, with 'Spirit' as an addition. Earth is represented by a yellow square, Air by a blue circle, Fire by a red triangle, Water by a silver crescent and Spirit by a black oval. The technique is to visualise one as being large enough to enable the practitioner to 'walk' into another world.

More advanced exercises using the Tattwas involved correspondences with the Temple directions, the magical weapons upon the altar, and even the seasons of the year. When such meditations took place in the 'Vault' – the temple that had been constructed at Isis-Urania – the awesome surroundings encouraged the success of the whole meditative process. Appropriate dress and symbolic artefacts, related to the specific intention of the journey, were also employed to full effect.

Once initiates were successful in gaining access to the Inner Planes, they were encouraged to recall their experiences to a scribe, a member of the Order appointed for that purpose. As well as magical formulae, many of these accounts of transcendental experiences were collected in the 'Z' documents of the Outer Order of the Golden Dawn. It was insisted that astral travellers were discerning upon their voyages, they were instructed upon how to recognize genuine teachers on the Inner Planes. Learning to trust the Higher Self so as to indicate the desirability of actions in the Inner and Outer Worlds was encouraged.

Initiation in the Second Order was considered to be a great honour. Westcott, in his meticulous fashion, even penned, 'The Conditions Needed for Entry into the Second Order'. It is a rather pious piece, but perhaps no more so than his usual efforts. One section is worth relaying as it makes mention of the aspirations of the would-be practitioner.

...the paths are many but there is one goal to which all good paths lead. Many paths are good, and end in happiness which is Wisdom; but every good path is toilsome, steep and often rugged; and if you find yourself treading a path of thought and action which is pleasant and easy – Beware thereof, and take counsel with your Higher Self, lest your self and you are but wandering in a labyrinth...[83]

Members of the Second Order were expected to comprehend the system of Enochian magic, as it was interpreted by Mathers. He insisted that the 'letters have more magical virtue than the common Hebrew, or English letters'. Second Order members were expected to be conversant in the Enochian language.[84]

Participating in the 'Portal Ceremony' meant passing from the First into The Second Order – the 'Inner Sanctum'.[85] This entitled the initiate to participate in ritual magic. It is important for those unfamiliar with the nature of a magical ritual to stress the potency of the proceedings. The language used, often archaic, is delivered in manner that encourages the particular mindset necessary to bring about the desired result. This approach, along with special costumes, gestures and the use of sacred objects combine to produce the required ambiance. A religious ceremony such as a Catholic Mass involves the same principles but, being of a public nature, cannot entirely reflect the intensity of a magical ritual.

A location for a temple where the Portal Ceremony could be enacted had been found. The construction of a suitably impressive interior was then planned, mainly by the Mathers. 'The Vault', as it came to be known, was in Thavies Inn, off the Holborn Circus in Central London. These premises were probably owned by Westcott, who later changed his mind about hosting the project. The Vault was then relocated to a less salubrious neighbourhood of London – Clipstone Street, off Great Portland Street.

The wooden frame of the Temple was constructed by a professional joiner, but the decoration was solely the work of the Mathers. 'The Vault' was a seven sided chamber, with a rose on the ceiling, and an immense red dragon on the floor. A more detailed description tells that,

> The vault was some twelve feet across, roofed and with panels of eight feet by five feet, each of which was divided into forty squares, each bearing a different symbol and painted in the appropriate colours....an elaborately painted pastos (or coffin) stood upon a moveable circular altar inscribed with the Hebrew letter *Shin* and the symbols of the four Cherubim of Ezekiel.[86]

The Hebrew *Shin* represents rebirth and has a correspondence with the Tarot card of 'Judgement'. In this familiar image, the souls of the dead rise towards redemption. The four cherubim are more commonly known as the four Apocalyptic Beasts: the Lion, Ox, Eagle and Man. The 'forty squares' were actually a 49 X 49 pattern – the 'Enochian Tablets'. This system was an essential part of the Second Order teachings.

The *Adeptus Minor* Ceremony was one of the most important rituals of the Order. Mathers, the architect of the ritual, wished to integrate the Rosicrucian and Egyptian schools of magic and the ritual reflects these influences. Twenty or so candidates passed through a 'portal' which from existing illustrations, seems to have resembled the entrance to a pharaoh's tomb. Two columns were inscribed with various hieroglyphs and the lintel bearing the most sacred symbols of Egypt – the Ankh, the Scarab, the Lotus Wand, and Ra himself. Above all was the Wadjet, the winged serpent and great symbol of protection. The Egyptian culture itself was around rebirth.

This 'passing through the veil' was an intrinsic feature of rituals performed in the Temples of Isis in ancient Egypt. Mathers saw himself as Osiris and so he believed that his presence at the ceremony was essential. The Rosicrucian Temple, it seems, existed only on the Inner Planes. Thus by combining it with the Egyptian theme of 'life through death' Mathers had created a ritual that combined both the physical and astral levels.

In Qabalistic terms the ceremony represented passing through the *Veil of Paroketh* – that of Illusion- in order that the soul may realise itself in the 'real' world. 'Reality' was seen as a spiritual state as opposed to a material one. To attain enlightenment any attachment to the physical world must be abandoned. The symbolic death and resurrection of Christian Rosencreutz was another model for gaining the new personality. During the ceremony, accounts of the sacrifices of Osiris and Rosencreutz were related to the initiate. A curtain was then drawn back and the Inner Temple was revealed.

As if the spectacle of the Vault was not enough, the culmination of proceedings was the spectacle of Mathers in splendiferous robes rising from the pastos. Even Waite, used as he was to grandiose Masonic rituals, was impressed by the ceremony. Considering his strict adherence to Christian principles, his praise of Mathers' ritual was fulsome.

> It could not be denied that the culminating Grade, as the system was then developed, had the root matter of a greater scheme than had ever dawned in the consciousness of any maker of Masonic Degrees under any Grand Lodge or Chapter, Conclave or Preceptory, in the whole world.[87]

The texts of the actual rituals performed by the Golden Dawn may be found in Israel Regardie's *The Golden Dawn*.[88] These, of course, cannot give us a true impression of the spectacle as it may have been. We are left to imagine these occasions as being the pinnacle of Mathers' achievements as a magician. Never again would he achieve these heights. At this point in his career he was, as all practioners wish to be, a true 'magus' – a master of magic.

VIII

Christian Mystic

Brother Waite warns us against the dark alleys that lead nowhere, and the false light that lead to ruin...he has come to draw a sharp line between the occult and the mystical, and therein he is wise.

Fort Newton

One who came to embrace Freemasonry to a much greater extent than either Mathers or Westcott, was Arthur Edward Waite. An American, Waite was brought up in the Catholic faith. The Christian Church and a love of its associated ritual never deserted him. At the outset Waite used Freemasonry for his own ends, later incorporating the Craft into his overall view of occult societies.

For a time Waite dallied with spiritualism and the Theosophical Society. He gradually developed a genuine interest in the occult, publishing a book on Eliphas Levi in 1886.[89] Waite joined the Golden Dawn in 1891. His motto was *Sacramentum Regis* ('The sacrament of the King'). The move is surprising knowing Waite's subsequent antipathy to the Egyptian gods and the Qabalah. He soon began to feel uncomfortable, saying, 'I began to hear things which...told me I should be well out of the whole concern',[90] and quit after a short time. He rejoined in 1896 and entered the Second Order in 1899. Waite always demonstrated a certain amount of levity in his dealings with Westcott. This is hard to imagine as any sense of humour is not overtly apparent in any of his writings.

Waite had an insatiable appetite for ritual and became dissatisfied with ceremony in the Golden Dawn, perhaps because Mathers was not supervising the occasions. Secret rites seem to have been Waite's lifeblood. His motive for rejoining the Freemasons was to gain knowledge of the 'Holy Royal Arch', a rite only open to Rosicrucians.

In 1898, while still involved with the Golden Dawn, Waite founded a Martinist Order in England. Based on the philosophy of Louis Claude de Saint-Martin, the venture was promoted by the French occultist, Papus. Realising that the move had not achieved the intended goals he sought, Waite later withdrew himself from Papus' influence.

Waite was a self-taught scholar. Pedantry and an intellectual superiority mar the pages of nearly all of his work. He had a horror of the popular, or the 'vulgar', as he would have put it. Perhaps for this reason he liked to parade his learning in overblown sentences and dense prose. Crowley had no time for him at all, satirising him as the ridiculous 'Artwate' in *Moonchild*. Israel Regardie also disliked him, describing Waite as, 'a pompous, turgid Roman Catholic masquerading in occult dress.'[91]

That said, his reputation has survived while that of many of his contemporaries has not. Waite published, along with Blavatsky, his own 'Secret Tradition'. R.A. Gilbert felt Waite was memorable,

...because he was the first to attempt a systematic study of the history of western occultism – viewed as a spiritual tradition rather than as aspects of proto-science or as the pathology of religion.[92]

Waite saw his mission as restoring Rosicrucian principles – to him a simple set of moral rules – to magical societies. He achieved this when the Golden Dawn disbanded in 1903 and he formed the I.R.G.D. – *The Independent and Rectified Golden Dawn*. During his life Waite created various other orders and always found ways to integrate his inner life into the rituals he superintended.

In 1901, he was initiated into The Runymede Lodge in Wraysbury, Buckinghamshire. He became a Master Mason in 1902 and attempted to mix the old Golden Dawn rituals that had been practised in the 'Vault' with those of Freemasonry. He persuaded Percy Bullock to join the Lodge in order to aid him in this ambition. He also attempted to persuade some Masons to join his own I.R.G.D. The number of Masonic affiliations that Waite accrued for himself in the period from 1902 to 1920 is astonishing.

To Waite, who collected a veritable cornucopia of occult honours, the 'Rectified Rite' was the prize he sought. An archaic ritual still available to a particular kind of enthusiast, Waite yearned to participate in this ceremony. The attraction was that he would then be installed as a member of the Knights Templar. Waite was more interested in acquiring this esoteric honour than in jockeying for political power within the Grand Lodge.

Waite's belief, that there was 'Masonry behind Masonry' consumed much of his thinking and research. His other passion, for spreading the Christian faith, was more direct. Much occult writing even up until the 1950s contains an apologia to Christianity, but Waite attempted to incorporate what he called *Christology* in his occult system. Waite espoused a view that the relationship between the divine and the human was personified in Christ. This is a basic tenet of Christianity, and Waite was always far more comfortable in his esoteric activities when familiar doctrines were within easy reach.

One artefact that would not have existed without Waite, or indeed the Golden Dawn, was the Rider-Waite Tarot deck. The most celebrated of all Tarot designs, the pack was drawn and painted by Pamela Colman Smith. In an overdue recognition of the artist's achievement, this Tarot is now usually referred to as the 'Waite-Smith' deck. The legacy left to us by this remarkable artist, a hundred years ago, is one of unsurpassed beauty and insight.

Smith was already an established artist when she was commissioned by Waite to produce the Tarot designs. Her work, although rooted firmly in the Decorative Edwardian style, is still accomplished and compelling. In 1899, she had published four books, *The Golden Vanity- Green Bed, Widdicombe Fair, The Annancy Stories* and *In Chimney Corners*. Smith later provided illustrations for Bram Stoker's *Lair of the White Worm*.

She was an original and exotic figure, even in a time when many personalities could be described as such. The writer Arthur Ransome has left us a detailed account of her home.

The walls were dark green, and covered with brilliant-coloured drawings, etchings, and pastel sketches. A large round table stood near the window, spread with bottles of painting inks with differently tinted stoppers, china toys, paperweights of odd designs, ashtrays, cigarettes boxes, and books; it was lit up by a silver lamp, and there was an urn in the middle of it, in which incense was burning.[93]

Pamela Colman Smith became a member of the Golden Dawn in 1901, being introduced to the Order by W.B. Yeats. Her motto was *Quod Tibi id Allis* ('To yourself as to others'). As a result of the 1903 split in the Golden Dawn, Smith followed Waite into his Independent and Rectified Order. Little, if anything, is known of her progress there. During her sojourn of eight years she did not pass beyond the first grade, and finally left the Order in 1910. During this time she met Florence Farr. An encounter in New York in 1907 began their friendship. It was the catalyst for the Tarot project.

Who determined the elements that would be included in the Tarot designs? Contributions may have been forthcoming from other Golden Dawn members and associates, namely Florence Farr, Yeats and Arthur Machen. However, it was Waite who ultimately decided upon the symbols that were to be included in the Major Arcana. Considering his spiritual stance, it is surprising that only a few of these are overtly Christian. In a surprising departure, the traditional title of card V, 'The Pope' was altered to 'The Hierophant', and most telling of all, card II, 'The Papess' became 'The High Priestess'. Here, Waite was obviously influenced to some degree by the magical writings of Eliphas Levi, but what occultist in the nineteenth century was not?

Waite seemed to be much more concerned with the writings he had put together to accompany the new cards when they went on sale than their designs. These works, issued by the Rider company, *The Key to the Tarot* (1910) and, *The Pictorial Key to the Tarot* (1911) were detailed instructions for methods of divination. Apart from the innovation of the 'Celtic Cross' spread, Waite's interpretations and methods can be safely ignored. Any understanding of the Tarot as a philosophical treatise, or a gateway to magic is completely ignored in these very pedestrian works.

Despite joining Waite's Order, Smith's loyalty did not always run to following his instructions for the Tarot. This is particularly evident in her designs for the Minor Arcana. This was only the second occasion that an attempt had been made to illustrate the fifty-six cards. The previous practice was simply to show the relevant number of wands or swords, for example, in some geometrical pattern. The *Sola Busca* Tarot of the fifteenth century had attempted to present individual images but, with a few exceptions, they are not very elaborate. Smith was obviously familiar with this pack however, as she adapted the *Three of Swords* and the *Ten of Wands* from this source.

We may say that the Rider Tarot contains more Colman than Waite. Her depiction of 'The Fool', with his splendid outfit is a masterpiece and has never been bettered. The cards of 'The Magician' and the 'High Priestess' are also superbly imagined. The Latter has a Qabalistic correspondence if examined carefully – the Tree of Life may be superimposed over the figure to reveal many of its secrets.

Astrological symbols found their way into the designs – rams' heads, bulls' heads and lions are featured. Smith herself was also drawn to Egyptian imagery. A sphinx appears on the 'The Chariot' card and Anubis appears on 'The Wheel of Fortune' card. When he saw the designs, Brodie-Innes, with his characteristic nit-picking, was inclined to carp. He criticised both Smith's scholarship, and what he saw as an obsession – 'with natural enthusiasm (she) was apt to see Egypt everywhere'[94]. Thankfully his criticisms were not acted upon.

There is a preponderance of towers in Smith's designs. In a lyrical explanation the artist confided,

> I often see towers white and tall standing against the darkening sky, those tall white towers that one sees afar topping the mountain crests like crowns of snow. Their silence hangs so heavy in the air that thoughts are stifled. The watchers' hands are lifted up to warn those wayfarers who wander idly. But he who knows the way, but gives the sign and enters in towards that sacred way.[95]

During her artistic training Smith had flirted with the notion of creating images inspired in her inner mind while listening to music. Debussy was her favourite composer for this exercise, and the two once actually met. He complimented Smith on what was to him a pleasing depiction of his music. She developed this method to the extent of genuinely experiencing synaesthesia – the ability to know one sense through another. Smith attempted to explain the sensations she felt when this happened.

> They are not pictures of the music themes – pictures of the flying notes – not conscious illustrations of the name given to a piece of music, but just what I see when I hear the music – thoughts loosened and set free by the spell of the sound.[96]

In 1911, she converted to the Roman Catholic faith. As a 'Modern Woman' she later supported the Suffragette Movement and designed posters for the cause.

Although she may have been disillusioned with the commercial aspect of both the art and publishing world, Pamela never ceased to believe in her abilities, or in the worthiness of her art. Her personal effects contain many scraps of paper covered with drawings and doodles, and even her church missal is sketched on in the margins and upon the flyleaf. Smith was always busy with pencils and sketchbook,[97] but she was to have very little material gain from her work. She died in penury in a remote part of England, and her possessions were used to pay her debts. Such was her fate, but her legacy is immeasurable and scores of Tarot readers and occultists are indebted to her for the images she created.

IX

A Divided Path

The time, which I have once or twice warned you of, is rapidly drawing near when you are to learn by bitter experience – for you refuse to learn by any other way – there are certain things of enormous power that do not enter into your present Philosophy.
W.T. Horton

The year 1896 was a tempestuous one for The Golden Dawn. Already rocking at its foundations, the whole edifice seemed about to collapse at any moment. The first crisis was precipitated by a prominent member of the London Lodge. As early as 1892, Dr. Edward Berridge had become a force in the Golden Dawn, becoming *sub-imperator* in that year. Crowley described him as, 'an ill-reputed doctor on the borders of quackery'.[98] He had a reputation within the Order of being able to bring about cures on the astral plane. How he brought these about is not known. On a more physical level Berridge advocated medical methods of an intimate nature. His public dissertations about his practices began to cause discord among the ranks of the female members.

His misdemeanour was to publicly advocate views on sex which were regarded by many in the Order as 'unwholesome'. Berridge was a devotee of Thomas Lake Harris, a therapist who advocated a 'sexual-pneumatic philosophy' in relationships. Berridge was a particular ally of the Mathers and it may be that his advocacy of 'Carezza', sexual intercourse without movement or orgasm, found favour with him. Moina also championed Berridge. Annie Horniman, on the other hand, had a deep antipathy to him, and this antagonism would soon develop into a full-scale quarrel.

The moment came when Horniman felt the situation could no longer be ignored. Several senior members, many women among them, had objected to Berridge's bizarre sexual teachings, his innuendos, and his forward manner. Horniman took it upon herself to be the spokesperson for those disturbed by Berridge's behaviour. When she complained to Mathers, she forgot to take into account Mathers' inability to consider any viewpoint other than his own. Mathers' did not consider Berridge had acted improperly when he received the complaints from Horniman. He responded with a voluminous correspondence, indicating that it was not Berridge who was at fault, but her. Mathers made a vituperative personal attack on Annie Horniman, accusing her of 'hereditary mania', 'intense conceit' and worse.

Her antipathy to Berridge was not the only thing troubling Horniman. While her loyalty to Moina did not falter, she was acutely aware of Mathers' mental state and was convinced that he was becoming increasingly unhinged. She knew that he had developed an appetite for the vagaries of political intrigue. In the Paris apartment he regularly entertained deposed royalty, 'Frenchmen and Spaniards whose titles were shadowy' [99] and other hangers-on. He was drinking even more heavily and entertaining lavishly, and all at Horniman's expense. The more Mathers' pretensions to hob-nobbing with the not-so-great increased, so did the sums of money that Annie bestowed upon him. It was unlikely that the situation could continue for much longer, particularly as the Mathers had now quarrelled with their patron.

Previous to all this, Mathers had demanded that members of the First and Second Order send him in writing an 'absolute submission to [his] authority'. Horniman had not done so and Mathers told her that other senior members had willingly complied with his request, although there is no evidence to verify his claims. Mathers was convinced that an insurrection, instigated by Horniman was about to take place.

Considering himself provoked beyond all reason, he laid down the law in no uncertain terms – 'I refuse absolutely to permit open criticism of, or argument concerning my actions in either Order, from you or any other member.' Mathers then completely lost his senses and made what was to prove to be the worst possible move – he expelled Horniman from the Order. Almost immediately, trouble came crashing about his head. How could he have expected otherwise? One can only surmise that his mania had reached such a peak that he believed he could issue any directive to members of the Order and it would be meekly obeyed by every member.

The first person to become involved in the Horniman affair was F.L. Gardner. He and Mathers had endured a strained relationship from the start. Gardner was a successful businessman and had offered to finance publication of an edition of *The Book of the Sacred Magic of Abra-Melin the Mage*. He had advanced Mathers a sum of money and had seen little in the way of return. When questioned about this Mathers responded with angry and threatening letters. His sponsor had reacted with admirable restraint.

Gardner seems to have been an autocratic individual, almost the match of Mathers. Perhaps this was in his favour, but his professional relationship with Florence Farr, who was Superintendent of Rituals, had also become difficult. It was strained to the breaking point the following year. Farr had sent him a somewhat testy communication, as this excerpt from the same shows.

Your manner to candidates, and those below you in the Order is intolerably rude; and I have over and over again received complaints from those who have been pained by your want of consideration for their feelings and your own dignity.[100]

If the above had been written by Annie Horniman perhaps no one would have been surprised by the officious tone. It seems that on occasion Farr was also capable of asserting her authority in a gratuitous manner. The effect of the letter was to hurt and humiliate Gardner who had previously considered Florence Farr to be a friend as well as a colleague.

Gardner had now received a communication from Paris mentioning, among other matters, the Horniman affair. Mathers protested that he would 'not permit longer her continued insubordination' *(sic)*. Gardner did not concur with Mathers' decision and organized a petition to reinstate Horniman. Although he received many written assurances of support, he did not forward these to Mathers. While promoting the petition, Gardner learned that Mathers would not entertain any plea on Annie's behalf.

Westcott was informed of the situation and his response was predictably flabby. He meekly protested to Horniman that he was forced to acknowledge Mathers' authority and thus could do nothing. The former founder was still terrified of Mathers. 'I shall be open to violent attack by him and I shall have to suffer his persecution', he wailed. Westcott insisted to anyone who would listen that Mathers was, 'more high up than I am, and I have no power to prevent any action of his'.

To cover himself, if Mathers accused him of anything else, Westcott had obtained an affidavit from T.H. Pattinson of the Horus Temple at Bradford. This document, which commented on the personality of both Mathers and Westcott, is basically an indictment of the former and a vindication of the latter. Pattinson wrote, 'I consider Mr. Mathers' mental state to be a peculiar one', and 'Dr. Westcott was, and still is, a clear headed man of business and an earnest literary student'.

Perversely, there were those who supported Mathers' decision for the removal of Horniman. Two prominent members of the Order with this view were Allan Bennett and J.W. Brodie-Innes. The former was an associate and mentor of Aleister Crowley. An extremely devout individual, he was only the second westerner to be ordained as a Buddhist monk. When Crowley rejected Buddhism, their friendship had come to an end.

In a rather ill-spirited letter to Gardner, Bennett described Horniman as a 'woman of wealth and leisure'. This comment followed on from Horniman revealing to those in the Order the details of the total bounty she had provided for the Mathers.[101] Bennett seemed to conveniently ignore the fact that if Horniman had not been a woman of some wealth, Mathers would not have been able to devote time to his magical researches, nor would the Order have continued for the length of time it did.

Brodie-Innes and his rather fawning wife were ardent, if not sycophantic, supporters of Mathers. They wrote in pompous terms to Gardner referring to Mathers as the 'Supreme Ruler in the Order'. Brodie-Innes suggested that 'it would be an unwarrantable presumption on my part to interfere with the jurisdiction of my superiors.' He ended his correspondence with the extraordinary statement – 'The King can do no wrong'.

Although Mrs. Felkin put her name to the petition, Dr. Felkin (*Fenim Respice* – 'Have regard to the end') did not, and neither did Percy Bullock (*Levivi Oculos* – 'I will lift up mine eyes'). These two – Felkin and Bullock – were to play a part in a new version of the Order which would rise in the wake of Mathers' eventual exit in 1903. Despite each of them having a strong personality, did both end up being a foil to Waite and Brodie-Innes?

In the following year, 1897, Mathers took it upon himself to summarily discipline Dr. Berridge, suspending him from both the First and Second order for a period of three months. There is no record of the doctor's reaction to this, or indeed any comment by Annie Horniman. It seems apparent that Florence Farr had no liking for Berridge either and that most of the members cared little for his fate within the Order.

The next blow to fall was the resignation of Westcott, Vice Imperator of Isis-Urania. Westcott was 'Coroner of the Crown' and the authorities, learning of his membership of the Golden

Dawn, did not consider such activities suitable for an officer of the court. Westcott wrote to Gardner explaining that,

> It had somehow become known to the State Officers that I was a permanent official of a society in which I had been foolishly posturing as one possessed of magical powers...[102]

Crowley's witty comment was, 'Did they further intimate to Dr. Westcott that he was paid to sit on corpses, not to raise them...'[103] This was not the first time that Westcott had been admonished by the authorities for his extra curricular activities. He referred to this episode in the same letter to Gardner, mentioning that there had been,

> A similar intimation in 1889 about the T.S. and my support of Madame Blav[atsky]...I had to cease lecturing there on Thursdays. I was then Vice Pres. of Blav. (sic) Lodge.[104]

The question of whether Mathers deliberately informed the authorities of Westcott's activities has never been satisfactorily answered. Howe believes it was highly likely that Mathers covertly informed them. He may have hatched the plan in Paris and then carried it out in some clandestine manner. Whether he was involved in the ousting of Westcott or not, Mathers was now the sole authority in the Golden Dawn. Naturally, this new burst of power unhinged him even more, as we shall discover.

Effectively, Westcott did not involve himself with Golden Dawn business after his resignation. He seemed to live in constant fear that Mathers would harass him, but this did not actually happen. Whether consciously or not, Westcott had always played the role of a scapegoat in Mathers' world. It was always too easy for Mathers to apportion blame to him for anything that went wrong in the Order.

Shortly before he died in 1925 Westcott wrote to Gardner

concerning the Secret Chiefs. He appears to be acknowledging their presence at one time, but implies their time has gone.

I see no reason to think that any supra-normal beings or Masters have divulged any secret knowledge for the last ten years at least.[105]

In November, 1898, Aleister Crowley was initiated into the Golden Dawn. His motto was *Perdurabo* ('I will endure'). Much has been written about Crowley, but for those not familiar with his significance as a magician and as a notorious figure of the twentieth century, it will be as well to provide the salient details of this extraordinary life.

Crowley was born in 1875, the year of the founding of the Theosophical Society, an occurrence which he considered significant and one to which he often referred. Even without his magical ventures, Crowley would have probably earned himself a reputation as a singular figure in the Edwardian era. He was an accomplished mountaineer, counting the world's major peaks among his achievements, an exceptional chess player, and a lyrical poet.

His writing on magic contains some of the best explications ever attempted upon this difficult subject, and he was certainly more than familiar with its principles. The strength of his dedication to raja yoga and meditation was exemplary, and his powers of concentration were quite astonishing. He never flinched from attempting to complete successfully any magical task, and his will was one of iron. It is the strength of character that separates the exceptional magician from his rivals, and Crowley was certainly a unique occultist.

Unfortunately his overweening ego drove him to indulge any desire that came his way, and many of the pleasures could only be described as depraved. His dealings with women amount to a reprehensible record of neglect and outright cruelty. Crowley always chose a partner with obvious psychic ability and many of his most impressive magical workings could not have taken place without their contribution. Regrettably, Crowley did not acknowledge their worth, and his chauvinistic attitude was at odds with the *zeitgeist*.

We shall refer to Crowley's further escapades in another part of our study. At this point we are only concerned with his impact upon the Order, which was dramatic but brief. When he became a member of the Golden Dawn, Crowley was less than enamoured with his fellow members, dismissing them with an alliterative contempt as, 'muddled middle-class mediocrities.' He made an exception for a few, including Alan Bennett, who he met after a ceremony and subsequently employed as a magical partner. Crowley never made a habit of disguising his animosities. He loathed Yeats, describing him as,

...a lank dishevelled demonologist who might have taken more pains with his personal appearance without incurring the reproach of dandyism.[106]

Crowley was respectful towards Florence Farr but was secretly dismissive of her, '...abilities were so inferior to her aspirations'.[107] He was also scathing about the instruction he received in his first 'Knowledge Lecture', demeaning the quality of its content, suggesting that 'any schoolboy in the lower fourth could memorize the whole lecture in twenty-four hours.'[108] Despite this, Crowley's advancement in the Order was rapid and by May of the next year he was knocking at the doors of the Second Order.

He had been conducting his own magical researches away from the Golden Dawn and, having obtained a copy of Mathers' *Abra-Melin* manuscript, was determined to embark upon the 'operation' himself. Crowley had private means – funds left to him from the sale of the brewery his family had once owned. By the Christmas of 1899 he had moved out of London and had discovered a secluded house in Boleskine on Loch Ness, the perfect venue for any magical experiments.

By 1897 the number of initiates into the Temples of the Golden Dawn totalled three-hundred and twenty-three and the total was nearer four hundred by 1900. If it had not been for the calamitous events that occurred in the first six months of that year, the Order might have continued. Morale was not high among the senior members, yet Mathers had become almost oblivious to any hints of a growing unrest among in the Isis-Urania Temple. As it was, the Golden Dawn never did recover from the shocks it was shortly to receive.

Mathers' lackadaisical attitude may have been caused by events unfolding in Paris, ones that directly concerned him and Moina. It seems that Mathers had been commissioned to design and erect an 'Egyptian Temple of Isis' at the Paris Exhibition of that year. By all accounts, the completed display received great acclaim from the Parisians. He and Moina seemed poised to be recognized as the spiritual authority on Isis. Mathers was thus riding high, but even at this moment of triumph his nemesis was lying in wait for him, literally on his doorstep.

X

The End

**Some ten years before I came in touch with Mathers' organ-
isation there were wars and rumours of wars.**
Dion Fortune

In February 1900, a trio of visitors arrived in Paris from America.
They were apparently eager to make the acquaintance of
Mathers. Dr. Rose Adams, Theo Horos and his wife, Madame
Horos, duly presented themselves at 87 Rue Mozart. Of his
visitors, it was Madame who impressed Mathers most. To his
astonishment she introduced herself with the motto *Sapiens
Dominabitur Astris*. This was the secret title of Anna Sprengel and
this alone may have been enough to convince Mathers that this
stout, imposing woman was somehow the spirit of Sprengel.
And was she also the reincarnation of Blavatsky? Madame Horos
was a stout woman and she took pains to explain to Mathers that
her great physique was due to her having,

> ...absorbed Madame Blavatsky's spirit on the physical death
> of that lady and that had occasioned her swelling to such
> dimensions.[109]

Whoever Mathers believed she was, he welcomed Madame
Horos and her companions into his life, a decision he was to
bitterly regret.

Mathers was ecstatic about Madame Horos' great mediu-
mistic powers. and introduced her (as a foreign member of the
Golden Dawn) to the company at a meeting of the Ahathor
Temple. He then, rather foolishly, lent her copies of all the First
Order Rituals. Soon after, she disappeared taking Mathers'

documents with her. From Paris, she and her entourage went to South Africa. What outrages Madame Horos perpetrated there are not recorded, but it seems the authorities issued a warrant for her arrest.

She was next seen in London where she had been attempting to gain entry to the Order by harassing in turn, Westcott, Gardner and Percy Bullock. Gardner informed Mathers, who cannot have been pleased to hear that the Horos party had arrived in the metropolis, or more importantly at 'his' Lodge. The party was described by Gardner thus,

> ...a gentleman with a Yankee accent about 5 foot, 1 inch, clean shaven, fair silky hair, half bald on top of head, dark eyes, and pale face with a fat corpulent lady who remained below in a carriage.[110]

It seemed they had adopted new identities. Madame Horos now professed to be 'Swami Vive Ananda', while her companion was plain 'Mr. Cornish'. The third member of the original party seemed to have been lost on the way. Gardner, although engaging in conversation with them, was understandably reticent in offering information about the Order. Mathers' reply to Gardner's letter we would now classify as a prime example of 'conspiracy theory'.

> I have every reason to believe them to be the emissaries of a powerful body who have for some years been trying occultly (sic) to injure other occult orders than their own...They are persons to be ware (sic) of...[111]

Percy Bullock also encountered Mr. Horos and, in a letter to Annie Horniman, wrote that the couple told him, 'They hailed from the Temis Temple in India'.

The end came for the fraudsters when they were arrested in

London the following year. It emerged that Madame Horos had been posing as Blavatsky, using the name 'Madame Helena' and also promoting herself as a healer. She claimed to be able to initiate followers into 'The Order of Theocratic Unity', and also informed her devotees that she was a leader of The Hermetic Order of the Golden Dawn. How would Mathers have reacted to that if he had heard it!

It was revealed that the Horos couple had left a trail of thievery and fraud from America to Australia. In London they had used the Golden Dawn rituals stolen from Mathers to perpetrate their crimes. The most odious of these was to abduct and sexually abuse young girls, promising them in return for submitting to indecent acts they would receive 'the Spirit of Christ'. At their trial both Mme. Horos and her partner received severe sentences.

The scandal naturally resulted in a great deal of unwelcome publicity for the Golden Dawn. At the trial, documents were read out that were identified as extracts from the Neophyte Ritual. The Solicitor General announced that the text was 'most blasphemous'. As a result of the scandal, a significant number of members resigned. The most dramatic exit was by William Peck from the Edinburgh Order who Westcott informed Gardner, had 'burnt all his lectures, letters, jewels (and) robes'.

Mathers later confided to Aleister Crowley that he had been totally convinced of the legitimacy of Madame Horos. Mathers' credulity was not only extraordinary it was tragically misplaced. He told Yeats that he believed Madame Horos to be a powerful medium who was 'controlled by very great and high forces, but much more frequently by evil spirits.'[112] The later insight was perhaps nearer the truth.

The whole episode left Mathers and the Golden Dawn in extremely bad odour with the public and esoteric circles alike. The Order would never recover from the blow. If there had existed a deliberate campaign to discredit magic and magical societies at the outset of the twentieth century, its success could not have been bettered by the results of the scandal. The Golden Dawn was held up to ridicule and became the subject of squibs and innuendo throughout London, if not the entire country.

If that was not enough, the revolt that had been growing daily within the Order now came to a head. Her intuition had told Florence Farr that the storm was about to break. For some time the officers of the Isis-Urania had expressed a growing dissatisfaction with Mathers' leadership from afar. Crowley, if in the unlikely event that his opinion had been sought, would have suggested their rebellion was due to Mathers' increasingly anti-English stance.

Some members were in favour of Westcott being reinstated and being made the new leader of the Golden Dawn. When he was approached, the proposed candidate resolutely turned down their offer. The situation was one of total chaos, and when the rumblings of discord came to his notice, Mathers, as ever, reacted badly and foolishly. He did the worst thing he could possibly have done, namely to alienate his strongest ally, Florence Farr. Mathers, who must have gotten wind of the intentions of the pro-Westcott faction, accused Farr of attempting to set up a schism within the Order. Naturally, Farr was outraged at such a baseless accusation. Considering Mathers' sentiments to be an insulting comment on her loyalty to him, she promptly resigned.

Mathers then responded in an even more bizarre fashion, even by his own idiosyncratic standards. He wrote to Farr responding to her resignation in disingenuous terms; he did not retract his accusation concerning her, but merely attempted to justify it once more. He repeated his fears regarding a revolution with Westcott at the head.

The remaining content of his missive contained the real bombshell, and one can only wonder why Mathers' ignited it. It was *in toto* a denunciation of Westcott. Mathers must have been aware that its effect would be to strike at the very foundations of the Golden Dawn and all that it stood for. Mathers informed Farr that Westcott had fabricated the documents on which the Golden Dawn had been founded. The relevant passage in the letter is as follows.

He has NEVER been *at any time* either in personal or in written communication with the Secret Chiefs of the Order, he having *either himself forged or procured to be forged* the professed correspondence between him and them, and my tongue having been tied all these years by a previous Oath of Secrecy to him, demanded by him, from me, before showing me what he had either done or caused to be done or both.[113]

An astonished Farr realized that she now held the fate of the Order in her own hands. How she reacted at that moment can only be imagined. Not only must she have felt the great weight upon her of these revelations, the feeling of being totally deceived must have completely overwhelmed her. Endless questions came flooding into her mind. If what Mathers said was true, who was aware of the alleged deception? Had Mathers always known of it?

Farr reasoned that if the Order of the Golden Dawn was no more than an invention and a fraud, none of these speculations meant anything at all. She had personally initiated a great number of people into the Order. Mathers had 'struck at the very heart of the moral basis' of Florence Farr's life and beliefs. The remarkably sober quote is from Crowley.

She decided not to alter her immediate plans to travel to Dublin where she was to take part in a theatrical production, and duly departed. Although Mathers had asked her to speak to no one of his revelations, before she left she wrote to Westcott asking for some clarification of the situation. When she returned from Ireland his reply was awaiting her. In it, characteristically, he was evasive. He stated that the accusations were untrue, yet admitted he could not prove anything either way. By remaining neutral, he offered no help whatsoever.

Farr felt she was forced to make the revelations known and called a meeting of select members of the Order. Percy Bullock and Yeats were included in the committee of seven she duly summoned. It was decided that Bullock should write to Mathers asking for a confirmation of his accusations against Westcott.

Receiving no reply, Farr then convened a general meeting of members of the Second Order. It was decided that before any decision concerning the Order was ratified, Mathers and Westcott must once more be requested to communicate with the members. Yeats volunteered to call upon Westcott and ask for some explanation. When he did so, Westcott proceeded to hide behind a mask of legalese and told Yeats that 'his lawyer had advised him to abstain from any statement'. Westcott later wrote to Yeats whining that if he contradicted Mathers he would be 'open to violent attack' and 'suffer his persecution'. Mathers on the other hand was made of much sterner stuff and reacted to the committee in a manner that might have been anticipated. Conducting a ritual very much in the style of the grimoires he had been studying, he cursed them all. He evoked *Typhon* and *Set*, all the while 'calling upon these mighty devils to fall upon his enemies'.

Apparently oblivious, or unaffected, by Mathers' attempts at using sorcery against them, the Order now almost unanimously agreed that the Cipher Manuscripts were forged. In their opinion, Westcott's continuing refusal to hand over any paperwork for inspection confirmed this. The minutes of all their meetings were sent to Mathers who responded with a lengthy but largely meaningless diatribe. He increased his threats of retribution against the Order, informing them he intended to call upon the Chiefs. 'I shall formulate my request for the Punitive Current to be prepared' he announced convinced that the Chiefs would attack any members who disobeyed him. He announced in melodramatic terms that 'a deadly and hostile current of will' from the Chiefs would cause any of his opponents to 'fall slain or paralyzed without visible weapons, as if blasted by the lightning flash'. With typically English aplomb the members refused to quail at these imprecations.

Mathers' next move was to seek an ally. He now had none in the Order, so had to search elsewhere. Not content to stand by and let 'his' Golden Dawn be taken from him, he decided to appoint an agent to take care of any business in England. He believed he knew exactly the right man for the job – Aleister Crowley. By coincidence, or divine design, Crowley had just arrived in Paris on the run from a sexual scandal in Cambridge. He arrived in Montmartre seeking refuge with Mathers.

Even before this, Crowley had written to Mathers offering him his services. He was well aware that rebellion was in the wind. Crowley was also smarting from what he saw as a grave insult from Florence Farr. She had taken it upon herself to deny Crowley's application into the Second Order. Her refusal to recognize Crowley's initiation was largely prompted by objections to Crowley practicing sex magic, or Tantra. On being told of the members' views Crowley informed them all curtly that this was his method of contacting the higher planes. He did not gain a sympathetic audience. Farr had no objection to sex *per se*, but she considered that sex magic was not a practice that the Golden Dawn should encourage.

Crowley may well have found a willing partner for his sexual predilections with a Mrs. Elaine Simpson. Her motto was, ironically perhaps, *Donorum Dei Dispensatio Fidelis* ('God will give gifts to the faithful'). Their affair had not been as clandestine as Crowley had assumed. When the liaison was discovered, disapproval of Crowley gained even more momentum. There were also rumours of other, more perverse, sexual practices and even accusations of devil worship and blasphemy.

Elaine Simpson's mother, another Order member, may have

had some hand in Crowley's denunciation, informing Farr that Crowley was habitually using sex 'to gain magical power'. It is known that Crowley had no high opinion of Elaine's mother, describing her as, 'a mischief-maker, maudlin and muddle-headed'.[114] Nevertheless, she ensured that her daughter ceased to be involved with Crowley.

Mathers had no such scruples about Crowley's morals, and speedily initiated him into the Second Order. In Mathers' mind 'The Great Beast' was about to be the saviour of his empire. In the course of several days of deliberations, he gave Crowley his instructions. He was to appoint new leaders for Isis-Urania, seize the Vault, and obtain a signed pledge of loyalty from every Adept. Mathers must have been in an elated mood if he expected Crowley to carry out his wishes. He had not taken into account Crowley's own motives for agreeing to all this. Crowley believed that he would be appointed Chief Adept in Anglia as a reward for his services.

Crowley returned to London and set about putting his master's orders into practice. It is significant that Crowley's inter-vention would eventually hasten the committee's determination to suspend Mathers. Thus by involving Crowley, Mathers hastened his own demise. The forthcoming drama, with Crowley well suited to play the part of the Demon King, was about to begin.

Crowley's first move was to contact Elaine Simpson and enlist her help which he somehow managed to do. To gain entry to the Vault, Mathers had instructed Crowley to write to Dr. Berridge. It was subsequently arranged that the doctor would give Simpson the keys to the Vault, and the locks could then be changed. All this was achieved smoothly enough. Crowley managed to convince the landlord of Blythe Road that he had authority to enter the Vault and did so. Quite why he remained there is uncertain, unless it was an act of defiance on his part.

Two days later, Yeats and Florence Farr, having got wind of

what was going on, confronted Crowley at the Vault. The police were then summoned. The constables were confronted with the extraordinary sight of Crowley,

...in Highland dress, a black mask over his face, and a plaid thrown over his head and shoulders, an enormous gold or gilt cross on his breast, and a dagger at his side.[115]

The presence of the long arm of the law prompted Crowley to withdraw in some confusion. He then sought to take legal proceedings against Florence Farr, as the most senior member of the Second Order. This scheme floundered hopelessly when the case was thrown out of court. Crowley, sensing that victory was far from his grasp, withdrew from the ring. Did he really take all these goings-on seriously? One is reminded of the comment by Israel Regardie, once a secretary for Crowley, about Crowley's character. 'He may be an extravagant boaster, while slyly laughing both at the object of his boast and at himself for making it.'[116]

The Second Order Committee then inevitably took the decision to suspend Mathers, Dr. Berridge, Mrs. Simpson and her mother from the Order. It was decided that the Golden Dawn paraphernalia was to be gathered together and secreted safely somewhere else. This would hopefully remove the danger of any ritual equipment being appropriated by Crowley.

By the end of April, 1900, the Committee had decided to close the Isis-Urania Temple, although they would continue under the title of the Golden Dawn. To this end, they elected new officers with different titles. The principal members were Florence Farr (Moderator), Annie Horniman (Scribe) and E.A. Hunter (Warden). Yeats was an *Adepti Literati* responsible for Mystical Philosophy. When Mathers was informed of these new arrangements he refused to acknowledge them and suggested that these officers of the Order should resign.

Crowley returned briefly to Paris to see Mathers before departing for New York in June. Their friendship had rapidly cooled. Crowley was convinced that he was the more accomplished magician, and by the end of 1900, he was summing up Mathers' involvement with the Golden Dawn in the following words:

> ...a scholar of some ability and a magician of remarkable powers, (he) had never attained complete initiation: and further had fallen from his original place, he having imprudently attracted to himself forces of evil too great and terrible for him to withstand...He therefore by his subtle wisdom destroyed both the Order and its chief.[116]

Although always dismissive of those who fell out of favour with him, Crowley's remarks are pertinent. Mathers almost pathologically followed the path to his own destruction.

The Great Beast emerged from this debacle with his reputation yet more sullied in the eyes of the Order. His infamies were this time revealed by astral means. Yeats reported that Crowley had a victim, a lady who was his mistress and from whom he extorted large sums of money'[117] The Sphere Group, under Florence Farr, contacted Elaine Simpson's spiritual self and instructed her to leave Crowley with whom she was still in contact. She apparently obeyed this edict and later confided 'a tale of medieval iniquity' [118] concerning her now former lover.

It could be argued that Crowley learned much more from his involvement with the Golden Dawn than he cared to admit. Certainly his later involvement with Egyptian deities may well have been inspired by Mathers' predilection with Isis and Osiris. With his first wife Rose, Crowley invoked the aid of Thoth (and later Horus) at the Great Pyramid in Egypt. As a result of these rituals Crowley met Aiwass, his Holy Guardian Angel who was to dictate *The Book of The Law* to him. Crowley may have adapted some of the Golden Dawn rituals for his own purposes, and later, when he founded the A.A., he used a hierarchy of magical grades based on the Roscrucians.

Crowley considered himself to be a reincarnation of Eliphas Levi. As he was the most accomplished magician of recent times *ipso facto* he, Crowley, should automatically now inherit that title. He was certainly not a man who tolerated rivals and regarded other men as either camp followers, or potential enemies. His 'scarlet women' as he titled his female companions often suffered at his hands, and he meted out abuse equally to both sexes. Gurdjieff, a philosopher and no mean magician himself, met Crowley in 1925 and was one of the few who did not fall for his charm – exactly the opposite. He angrily dismissed Crowley from his home with many an insult.

Discord was now also the hallmark of the new regime in the Golden Dawn. It might have been that Mathers' curse was now taking effect. A rift between Annie Horniman and Florence Farr had suddenly become apparent. Horniman, now returned to the fold, was anxious to retain some semblance of unity within the Order. Misguidedly, she took against Florence Farr's Sphere group, deciding it was a divisive influence in the Order. To fully appreciate what was at the root of this particular schism, it is necessary to be aware of the magical approach to the Golden Dawn that each of them had adopted.

Like all of the senior members of the Order, Florence Farr wrote extensively on the theory of magic. Many of her ideas were very advanced for the time. When we consider that the following extract from 'On the Play of the Image-Maker' was written nearly one hundred years ago, it has more than a ring of current New Age thinking.

I do not think we sufficiently realise that our life is in reality a series of illusions. For instance, if we accept the delusion that we are healthy we overcome disease; if we are open to the delusion that we are unhealthy, we give way before disease. This individual susceptibility to notions and impulses is the really interesting aspect in the study of a human being. It does not arise from birthright and country. If it did twins would be identical.[119]

The intensity of her personal power can be sensed in the words. Of all the members of the Golden Dawn, Farr is the figure that emerges as the most suited to magical practice. But her conflict with Mathers had token its toll and she was on the brink of abandoning the Order. Farr was now inclined to return to her theatrical interests. If she was to remain an active member of the Golden Dawn, it was necessary to find a very strong reason within herself for doing so. With 'The Sphere' group she rediscovered her enthusiasm for ritual. Farr described her project as 'a strong nucleus on purely Order lines' – twelve members whose task was to 'concentrate forces of growth, progress and purification.'[120]

From the time she had been appointed by Mathers, Farr had been responsible for all the decisions made concerning the Second Order. She had set about changing the requirements for entering this part of the Order. The emphasis was to be on 'magical understanding', which could take the form of passing an oral examination rather than the strict academic requirements that had formerly been required. When Annie Horniman was reinstated in an executive role, she began by investigating the way that the Golden Dawn had been organised since the departure of Westcott.

The newly appointed 'Scribe' was horrified. Her strict sense of order was outraged by Farr's method, or lack of it. In a rather officious manner, she complained first to Yeats, attempting to convince him that Farr was incompetent. In addition, she also insisted that the Sphere Group was a dangerous threat to the stability of the Order.

The group certainly seemed to pose no such threat at all. Its *raison d'être* was an attempt at world healing. Working from their own homes, at a specified time the Sephiroth upon the Tree of Life was visualised by each of the twelve members. The images were projected, at first over the Vault at Blythe Road then gradually increased in size until they encompassed the city of London, the Earth, and finally the Solar System. The ultimate aim of the exercise was for each member to link themselves and the universe to the highest sphere – Kether. Powerful stuff indeed! Perhaps Annie Horniman, in her sanctum, pouring over piles of randomly filed Order records, could feel the vibrations.

For other activities in the Group, Florence Farr employed the personal knowledge she had gained from her links with Egyptian deities. Among other exploits, she had once invoked a serpent which led her to the Adytum of Isis. For some time the Sphere Group had wielded enormous influence in the Order as it was responsible for making regular divinations to gain insights into its workings. Discovering Mathers' current agenda had been one of their tasks, as they were then able to keep one step ahead of him.

Horniman's fears concerning the Sphere group were groundless, particularly as Farr had never intended to stand outside of the Order. It can only be surmised that an inordinate amount of resentment had gathered in Horniman's soul since her ousting from the Golden Dawn. With Mathers out of the way, her ill-temper was now directed at Farr and releasing a pent-up jealousy.

Farr's group had an Egyptian 'Master' who may have been Kha'muast, High Priest of Ptah, although Caroline Tully reminds us that,

The identity of Farr's 'Egyptian Adept' is contested. On the one hand, friends of hers to whom she left a wooden 'shrine' in which an Egyptian being allegedly dwelt claim that its name was Nemkheftka whereas on the other hand, eye-witnesses report that the name of the entity was Mut-em-menu." and " Mut-em-menu', a coffined mummy acquired by the British Museum in 1835, is a likelier candidate for Farr's 'Egyptian Adept'.[121]

Not all members of the Order were so enthusiastic about embracing Egyptian influences. In September of 1900, Farr reports in a letter to an unknown correspondent,

'You will understand that with the anti-Egyptian feeling about I shall still refuse to discuss Egyptian formulae with anyone not especially in sympathy with the ancient Egyptians.'[122]

In light of the choice of the names of Egyptian gods and goddesses for the various Golden Dawn Temples throughout England, this seems quite bizarre. Farr later wrote to Brodie-Ines early the following year, 'I soon found there was considerable prejudice against Egyptian Symbolism amongst the members of the Order.' Perhaps Annie utilized this prejudice in her attempts to discredit the Sphere Group.

With the new arrangements, Yeats' position was on a solely executive basis. Farr's magical authority, which was what counted, was greater than his. Annie Horniman now believed that if anyone had the right to lead the Golden Dawn, it was her. She was prepared to sacrifice everything, even friendship, in the pursuit of this ambition. Yeats was no match for Horniman and he rather weakly agreed to support her campaign.

Farr, suddenly aware of Horniman's intentions was scandalized. 'I discovered that my group which had been working quietly for three years was being violently attacked'.[123] Horniman was almost demented in her persecution of the Sphere Group and attempted to prevent them from actually meeting. It is not beyond the bounds of possibility that Annie then put together a magical group specifically for the purpose of attacking members of the Sphere Group on the astral planes, Farr in particular.

On a purely executive level, Horniman was not to get her wish. By dramatically accusing members of the Sphere group of 'evil' and 'pernicious practices in our Tomb [The ceremonial Vault]' she alienated herself from the Order Council. At a meeting in early 1901, the Sphere Group was officially permitted to continue their rituals and meditations without any administrative hindrance. During meditations in her Group, Farr had beheld some ominous visions. She became convinced that, even if she offered of peace and harmony to those in the Order who objected to her methods, little would be achieved. She was correct in her conclusions; the Golden Dawn had been shaken by so many rifts it could never function in the same way again.

After the excitement of Crowley's intervention into Golden Dawn affairs, much of what followed was an anti-climax. Little was now to be heard of magic or any transcendental matters within the Golden Dawn. Energy was diverted into what was little more than boardroom squabbles. Periodically the executive received Mathers' furious letters of objection to their proposals and they simply ignored him.

In May, 1902, a new constitution for the Golden Dawn was drawn up. The governing of the Order was given to Percy Bullock, Dr. Felkin and Brodie-Innes. Appointed for one year, these three were cited as 'The Three Chiefs'. On hearing of this, Mathers' communications rose to untold heights of invective. Addressed to 'the Rebels against my authority', his correspondence included a varied assortment of commands, threats of legal action, and dire warnings of occult revenge. His most astonishing accusation was that Madame Horos was an agent sent by the committee to entrap him! Mathers also insisted that Westcott was in complete agreement with his every word. If this was in any way true, then Mathers' mysterious hold over his former colleague had intensified even more.

When Mathers no longer led the Order, much was lost of the original intentions of the Golden Dawn. He was the main architect of the rituals used in the Second Order. The elements that gave Mathers' work its potency came from the Egyptian deities, the grimoires, and the rest of the great bulk of knowledge he had acquired. When others less committed to this amalgam of wisdom took over, the power that emanated from the Order was substantially weakened.

It is significant that Madame Blavatsky in her Theosophical Society, and Mathers in the Golden Dawn, both set such so much store on their 'guides', respectively, the 'Masters' and the 'Chiefs'. The Order stressed the need for the initiate to make contact with 'teachers' on the Inner Planes. Records of such contacts, made by Florence Farr and Annie Horniman, exist in the Flying Rolls.

With the virtual collapse of the original Golden Dawn, replaced by various factions hostile to each other, claims were made by various individuals as to having received 'divine directives'. Many of these were desperate attempts to legitimize, on a spiritual level, the wresting of power from others. Felkin and Brodie-Innes claimed to have made new contacts with otherworldly sources. For them, the 'Secret Chiefs' had been replaced by 'The Sun Masters', and one of the duties of Felkin was to report to Brodie-Innes the details of their communications.

The committee faced two problems. First was the status of Westcott who, in theory, was senior to them all. Second, Annie Horniman continued to complain in such detail and so variously that, in the end, no judgment passed by the Chiefs satisfied her. Realizing she would never be leader of the Order, she resigned at the beginning of 1903. Horniman retired from any involvement in magical activities and devoted her energies to her previous love, the theatre. In a fortuitous move, Yeats persuaded Horniman to go to Dublin and involve herself in productions there. She became so enthusiastic about her new role that in 1904 she bought a property which became the celebrated Abbey Theatre. She returned to England and financed the renovation of the Gaiety Theatre in 1908. It was thanks to Annie Horniman that the modern repertory movement in Great Britain was born.

Percy Bullock also resigned and Waite, seizing his chance, made an attempt to take over the Order. The ploy was not successful, only resulting in splitting the ranks even more. The outcome was that Brodie-Innes and Felkin formed the *Stella Matutina* and Waite, preferring to adapt the old organization, inaugurated the *Independent and Rectified Rite of the Golden Dawn*.

This order openly embraced Christian Mysticism. At the outset, Christian doctrine had not been popular within the Golden Dawn. To the modernists, the Church could never be freed of negative associations, its baneful influence still hanging heavy over Victorian England. Later it would emerge that some members of the Order who regarded divine power as being akin to the Christian God, were prepared to embrace Waite's principles.

Howe speculates that the motive of these three individuals were all entirely different. Waite wanted to remove all traces of Mathers' magical tradition; Brodie-Innes wished to preserve the authoritarian, academic aspect of the order; and Felkin was content to commune with the Secret Chiefs, whoever they might be. Alan Richardson is strongly of the opinion that,

'Felkin was a *real* magician, and closer to the spirit of Mathers than any of the other heretics who had parted company with their fellow leader.' [124]

In 1903, Crowley created a Third Order of the Golden Dawn – The *Argentum Astrum* – 'Order of the Silver Star'. He considered himself to be the legitimate heir to Mathers' legacy, although others actively questioned this premise. During the next decade, Crowley became more involved in another magical organization

– the O.T.O. (Ordo Templi Orietis). In 1912, he left the Golden Dawn behind completely and founded the magical commune of Thelema.

A series of bizarre episodes followed all this. The most extraordinary was the sight of Felkin embarking on a wild goose chase of incredible proportions. In early 1904, a letter arrived for him from a Fraulein Anna Sprengel. Its content was quite inconsequential, but it was enough to prompt Felkin to travel to Germany in 1906 in search of a woman he supposed was the niece of the founder of the Golden Dawn. He was not successful in discovering her but undaunted, he set off again in 1910 on the same mission. On this occasion his aim was to introduce Westcott, who happened to be travelling in Germany at the same time, to the celebrated Sprengel.

Felkin seemed determined to prove that the Sprengels, both aunt and niece actually existed. In this way he would forever exonerate Westcott from charges of having acted fraudulently when setting up the Golden Dawn. His investigations involved attempts to discover powerful Rosicrucian connections in Germany. Such a surreal set of goings-on is difficult to envisage. Westcott was being solicited to meet the real-life version of his own fantasy! Whatever the premise, the encounter did not happen, at least not on this plane. Felkin journeyed to Hanover but his plans were once more thwarted. It seems he decided instead to make do with visiting Rudolf Steiner in Berlin. Once back in England, he announced to one and all that he had been awarded Rosicrucian titles by Rudolf Steiner. We have only Felkin's word that this was true.

Brodie-Innes was having no part of Felkin's expeditions and departed to join the Amen Ra Temple in Edinburgh as a chief adept. At first, Felkin questioned his right to do so, but soon left Brodie-Innes to follow his own devices. Meanwhile, he continued with his European investigations. Felkin became so obsessed with his preoccupations that on a trip to Germany in 1914 he seemed unaware that war had been declared. Felkin and his wife were fortunate to get out of the Kaiser's Germany unscathed.

Felkin was either incredulous or unaware of a paper Waite had published about the Cipher Manuscripts several years before. In 1908, Waite had presented his findings about the Manuscripts in 'Historical Notes', which shed significant doubt about their authenticity. Waite had examined the documents with Wallis Budge, the renowned Egyptologist, and their conclusion was that,

...considerable proportions...were written on watermark paper of 1808...so prepared with intent to deceive and were not only subsequent to the discovery of the Rosetta Stone but were later than the publication of *Isis Unveiled*. [125]

But, ciphers or no, Felkin continued to wave the Golden Dawn flag. In 1916, he inaugurated the Hermes Lodge in Bristol, a city in the south-west of England.

Brodie-Ines was finally reconciled with Mathers in 1917 the year before the latter died. He wrote his reminiscences for the *Occult Review* in an article generous in its assessment of his former mentor.

MacGregor had all the Celtic fiery temper and pride of his race. He would pick a quarrel on a point of punctillo, a real, or even a fancied slight to his clan or his nation, and fight it out with the keen zest of a medieval knight, but always at a disadvantage, for he was above all a chivalrous Highland gentleman, and in his nature was not one grain of malice...Vanity doubtless he had, but it was the harmless vanity of a child. Credulous too, and liable sometimes to be taken in by an imprudent imposter, for he who hated deceit was slow to suspect it in another; but unsparing in his denunciation when he found it. [126]

S.L. MacGregor Mathers' death came on November 20, 1918, a victim of the outbreak of Spanish influenza that spread across Europe in the last year of the First World War. Almost nothing is known of his activities from 1903 onwards, although it is possible that the Aathoor Temple continued to function right up until Mathers' death. Did he take part in any ritual magic or was he content to continue with his own researches? How he and Moina managed to support themselves during this time is another unsolved mystery. One suspects they lived in abject poverty. It was a sad end for the founder of the most renowned and influential magical organization of recent times. His last letter ends with the telling sentiment, 'I am he who is robed in a body of flesh, but in whom doth shine the Spirit of the Gods.'[127]

After Mathers' death Moina returned to England, to live in London. It appears that she relied heavily on the charity of her former associates to establish herself in any comfort. Yeats' *Autobiographies* had recently been published. Reading it, Moina took great exception to his assertion that Mathers 'was to die of melancholia'. She and Yeats were later reconciled over this although he did not retract the statement in later editions of this work. Maud Gonne, one of the few people who visited the Mathers during the First World War, confirmed that Yeats' view was correct.

The London Lodge was not the only organization with which Moina was involved. R.S. Mead, a former luminary of the Theosophical Society, had founded the Quest Society which included Moina and Annie Horniman among the members. A description of Moina at this time reveals that,

...she looked like 'a witch', 'a gypsy', 'an Egyptian priestess' ...(and) spoke in a resonant voice that dominated the assembly ...[she] possessed a great calm which gave an impression of hidden power. She appeared taller than her actual height because of her upright carriage...Her hair had turned white.[128]

Wynn Westcott died in Durban, South Africa in 1925. His papers had been left in England, presumably in the London Lodge. They were housed in the famous 'black box' which over the years had acquired a reputation as being a treasure trove of great occult value. It was assumed by some that the truth about the founding of the Golden Dawn would finally come to light when it was finally unlocked. No such thing happened, when opened – it revealed nothing. It seems that Westcott's secrets, or lack of them, went with him to the Other Side.

XI

The Magical Heritage

...Arthur Machen seems to have come to the conclusion that the Golden Dawn was no more than a bad joke...
Francis King

Much had changed in the world during the fifteen years from the inception of the Golden Dawn to its demise. Those who had been involved in the Order were certainly older, but whether they were any wiser is a moot point. Several individuals were to take turns at the tiller of the vessel of magic, but it was now a rudderless craft. And who had the right to be captain of the ship? Two members of The Golden Dawn would emerge as great Magicians in the twentieth century, Dion Fortune and Aleister Crowley. This pair, with W.G. Gray, must be reckoned the leading lights of the occult in the last hundred years.

Each of the magical societies founded by Crowley might be seen as a 'School for Scandal'. Both the *Argenteum Astrum* (A∴A) and the *Ordo Templis Orientis* (O.T.O) with which he was involved stressed the importance of 'Sex Magick' in their rituals. Crowley's notoriety increased with the years, the last of his communal projects, extant from 1920-3 was the founding of the 'Abbey of Thelema' in Italy. During its brief existence it gained such a dangerous reputation that it was closed down on the orders of Mussolini.

Thelema – from the Greek noun 'will' – was the worldly manifestation of a personal philosophy of Crowley's. The Elements of Rabelais, the sixteenth century monk from who we derive the word 'Rabelaisian', and the notorious rake Sir Francis Dashwood, lurk in the more gross elements of Thelemic practices. The overtly Egyptian contribution is represented by

Nuit the goddess of the sky depicted as a naked figure arching over the Earth. She is the partner of Geb – the Earth – and mother of Isis.

Crowley saw himself as a prophet, and he still features prominently in many a personal myth among New Agers. The accusations of his being a 'Black Magician' hover about Crowley like a cloud of poison gas. The truth is that he had as much contempt for those who took part in a 'Black Mass' as any true magician would. Crowley certainly knew his magic and wrote extremely knowledgeably on the subject. As a man with a formidable intellect he always defended his corner vigorously. Away from the glamour of 'magick', he had some admirable traits as well as some really awful ones.

Crowley always felt he was the most appropriate person to carry on the magical heritage of the Golden Dawn. In 1925, he claimed that he was,

> ...invited to the H.Q. of one of the Secret Brotherhoods in Germany...The secret heads of other bodies joined us. The genuine representatives of H.P.Blav[atsky] were Otto Gebhardi and Martha Kuentzel. [I]...represented the secret councils of all the important Orders of the Great White Brotherhood. A general council...elect[ed] me as the Secret Head of all these bodies.[129]

The exhortation Crowley adopted to embody his later magical principles was – 'Do what thou wilt shall be the whole of the law'. The words became a kind of mantra in the 1960s, a time when all things magical were considered most chic. Its meaning has been largely misunderstood, being seen as an endorsement of total licence and anarchy, which is to totally miss the point.

The less well-known Crowley axiom – 'Every man and every woman is a star' – advocates that the individual follow their true destiny. In the first few decades of the twentieth century, such a sentiment would still have been seen as most radical, particularly for women. Such a stance is now almost a given. Crowley was certainly an advocate for change, even a catalyst of the 'modern movement', but a streak of perversity ran through all that he undertook.

Apart from his magical writings, his legacy must include 'The Book of Thoth', his idiosyncratic Tarot which incorporated Egyptian correspondences. The images, painted by Lady Frieda Harris, still have a fascination for many students of the occult.

Dion Fortune was initiated into the London Temple of the Alpha and Omega Lodge in 1919. She was not entirely impressed by its methods.

> Practical teaching from official sources was conspicuous by its absence...The glory had departed...and (it) was manned mainly by widows and grey-bearded ancients...[130]

Moina Mathers was Head Imperatrix and it was perhaps inevitable that she and Dion Fortune would not see eye-to-eye. Despite her initial disappointment with the Order, Dion still retained a respect for the original Golden Dawn.

> ...anyone with any psychic perceptions at all could not fail to realise that there was power in the ceremonies and formulae; and anyone who had made a study of them also speedily found out that in the system of correspondences taught in the GD they had got something of inestimable value.[131]

She took the motto *Deo non Fortuna* ('God not fortune') from which her name, Dion Fortune, came. She participated in much Golden Dawn business – too much for Mather's queen. Very soon after Dion had joined the Order, Moina took exception to the content of this new member's writings. Soon after, Dion was expelled for publishing books Moina considered were 'betraying the inner teaching of the Order'. Ostensibly the reason for her expulsion was that 'certain symbols' had not appeared in her aura after her initiation!

Dion took this move with reasonable grace, but Moina was not going to leave it at that. She set about employing all her magical powers to intimidate and frighten Dion, and in a singular manner. Dion's account of these incidents, although matter of fact, does not detract from what must have been a terrifying experience. What follows is a condensed account of a series of what were most definitely psychic attacks.

...I suddenly saw coming down the stairs towards me, a gigantic tabby cat, twice the size of a tiger. It appeared absolutely solid and tangible. I stared at it for a second and then it vanished. I instantly realised that it was a simalcrum, or thought-form that was being projected by someone with occult powers...[132]

The identity of this 'someone' was all too evident. An echo of this encounter occurred some seven or eight years later. Dion was forced into combat with her 'enemy' while travelling in the Inner Planes. She realized that her way was blocked by the figure of Moina herself.

She appeared to me in the full robes of her grade, which were very magnificent, and barred my entry, telling me that by virtue of her authority she forbade me to make use of these astral pathways.[133]

However, Dion was not the kind to back down to anyone. By using every ounce of her formidable will, she vanquished Moina and continued on to her astral destination. The sequel, on the earthly planes, was just as dramatic. When she undressed that same night, Dion discovered her body was covered in scratches from neck to waist – as if she had been mauled by a huge cat. The most extraordinary aspect of all this is that Moina Mathers had died eighteen months earlier. It seemed she still desired to hold sway from the other side of the veil.

Dion Fortune became, in the view of many, the greatest practioner of magic in the C20th. In 1922, with C.T. Loveday, she founded the *Fraternity of the Inner Light*. Many renowned occultists have been associated with this organization over the years. Col. Charles Seymour, Bill Gray, Christine Hartley, W.E. Butler and Dolores Ashcroft-Nowicki are the most notable. Dion clearly knew something about 'degrees of initiation' as these comments about inner guides reveals,

No rite is effectual unless these invisible beings are present. It is the knowledge of who they are and how their presence is obtained which constitute the real secret of a degree.[134]

Like Waite, Dion Fortune took a Christian approach to magic, but unlike him, she did so on her own terms. She nurtured a great love for Glastonbury in Somerset, England where she is buried. She described the place as the English Lourdes. Regarding the pagan and Christian forces that were present upon the Tor, Dion was always quick to point out that the one never entirely dominated the other.

The *raison d'être* of the Golden Dawn was to initiate practitioners of magic and the purpose of any initiation is to produce an incorruptible, pure individual. Promoting that aim can only be seen as highly admirable. Along with the visionary and the disciple, it attracted its share of megalomaniacs and charlatans. In any organization, when an over abundance of ego comes to rule, quarrels and conflict are inevitable. However, a magical society will, by its nature, have an astral existence concurrent with ordinary reality.

Magic is powerful force, one that eventually destroys those

who attempt to employ it for their own ends. Many who become involved with the occult do not understand this simple edict. The forces that make up the universe are mighty, and often terrifying. Mortal minds cannot comprehend the ways of creation unless they humble themselves before the gods and goddesses. All powers are there for man to use but for them to be revealed to him he must prove that he is pure of heart.

Was it possible that Mathers was himself the victim of forces beyond even his control? Did his work with ancient texts contribute to his megalomania? Were his curses on those who tried to wrest his leadership away from him effective? What is undoubtedly clear is that when the end of the Golden Dawn came he was the one who was to fall the furthest.

With hindsight it seems incredible that the Order lasted for as long as it did. We should regard the Golden Dawn as a glorious experiment that worked well – but for only a short time. It has left its legacy in the work of those serious students of magic who quietly continue about their business, and consult the magi of long ago. Such a phenomenon as the Golden Dawn still exerts a fascination upon us. We wander in Victorian Paris and London rubbing shoulders with the men and women who, all those years ago, made magic live and be glorious. That achievement can never be taken from them.

References

1. Dion Fortune, *Moon Magic* (New York: Samuel Weiser 1995) p. 96

2. G.I. Gurdjieff, *Flight from Reason* (London: MacDonald 1972) p.182

3. In Francis Barrett's *The Magus* of 1801, an advertisement appears offering 'private instructions and lectures' in 'Natural Philosophy, Natural Magic, the Cabala, Chemistry, the Talismanic Art, Hermetic Philosophy, Astrology...' Did this perhaps offer a template for the founders, one that was embraced?

4. Edward Maitland, *Anna Kingsford, Her Life, Letters, Diary and Work* (London: George Redway 1896) p.32

5. Occult Review 29 no.4, 1919 pp.196-199

6. Ithell Colquhoun, *The Sword of Wisdom* (New York: G.P. Putnam & Sons 1975) p.156

7. Ellic Howe, *Magicians of the Golden Dawn – A documentary history of a magical order* (London: Routledge and Kegan Paul 1972) p.34

8. R.A. Gilbert, *Revelations of the Golden Dawn* (Chippenham: Quantum Publishing 1997) p.76

9. Gilbert, p.82

10. Gilbert, p.73

11. Francis King, *Ritual Magic in England (1887 to the Present Day)* (London: Neville Spearman 1970) p.25

12. Howe, p.9

13. Howe, p.6

14. Arthur Machen, *Things Near and Far* (New York: Alfred A. Knopf 1923) p.27

15. Literally, a counterfeit cheque.

16. Machen, p.27

17. W.B. Yeats, *Stories of Red Hanrahan: The Secret Rose: Rosa*

Alchemica (London: Macmillan 1913) p.215.

18. Francis King, *The Golden Dawn – Official History* (London: Macmillan 1967) p.36
19. Howe, pp.129-130
20. Howe, p.131
21. R.A. Gilbert, *Golden Dawn Companion* (Wellingborough: Aquarian Press 1989) p.31
22. Howe, p.61
23. Greer, Mary K., *Women of the Golden Dawn* (Rochester, Vermont: Park Street Press 1995) p.75
24. Greer, p.222
25. Mathers, p.xiii
26. Alan Richardson and Geoff Hughes, *Ancient Magicks for a New Age* (Minnesota: Llewellyn Publications 1989) p.7
27. W.B. Yeats, *Autobiographies* (London: Macmillan 1955) p.187
28. Yeats, p.255
29. Greer, p.314
30. Susan P. Castera, *Images of Victorian Womanhood in English Art* (Rutherford N.J: Farleigh Dickinson University Press 1987) p.178
31. The 'Flying Rolls' were a collection of thirty-four manuscripts written 1892-1894 by members of the Order. They were sometimes used as the basis for lectures, at other times they simply remained records of astral experiences.
32. Flying Roll No. XVIII 'Progress in the Order'. The whole is quoted verbatim in King, p.111
33. The impression is borne out by Hesketh Pearson who was his biographer in *Bernard Shaw – His life and personality* (London: Methuen 1961). Pearson depicts Shaw, in his attitude to women, as an obnoxious tyrant.
34. Greer, p.154
35. Greer, p.155
36. Russell, p.58
37. Russell, p.117

38. E. Stephen Gwynn, *Tributes to the Memory of W.B. Yeats* (London: Macmillan 1940) p.15

39. Yeats, p.230

40. Ed. Stephen Gwynn, p.17

41. Joseph Hone, *W.B. Yeats, 1865-1939* (London: Macmillan 1943) p.156

42. Greer, p.158

43. Greer, p.373

44. Allan Wade (ed), *The Letters of W.B. Yeats* (London: Rupert Hart-Davis 1954) , p.210

45. Aleister Crowley, *Moonchild* (New York: Samuel Weiser 1975)

46. Hone, p.106

47. A. Norman Jeffares, *W.B. Yeats – Man and Poet* (London: Routledge & Kegan Paul 1949) p.110

48. Jeffares, p.134

49. Howe, p.100

50. Calculated to be the equivalent of $10,000 in today's currency.

51. S. Liddell MacGregor Mathers, *The Key of Solomon the King (Clavicula Salomnis)* (London: Routledge and Kegan Paul 1972) p.vii

52. Ibid, p.viii

53. Samuel Liddell MacGregor Mathers , *The Book of the Sacred Magic of Abra-Melin the Magi* (New York: Dover publications 1975) p.xv

54. Ibid., p.xvii

55. Ibid., p.xv.

56. Aleister Crowley, *Magic* (London: Routledge & Kegan Paul 1973) p.297

57. Dion Fortune, *Through The Gates of Death* (Wellingborough: Aquarian Press 1968) p.72

58. Flying Roll No.21 – King, p.153

59. Yeats, pp. 335-336

60. Ibid., p.337
62. Joseph Campbell, *The Hero With a Thousand Faces* (Princeton: Bollingen 1972) Footnote. p.88
63. Yeats, p.337
64. Ibid., p.339
65. Greer, p.153
66. Lucius Apuleius, *The Golden Ass –The transformation of Lucius* (London: Penguin 1958) p.98
67. Ibid, p.387
68. Mathers, p.ix
69. Greer, p.250
70. Russell, p.213
71. E. Wallis Budge, *Egyptian Religion* (New York: Dover Publications 1971) p.109
72. Naomi Ozaniec, *The Kabbalah Experience – The Practical Guide to Kabbalistic Wisdom* (London: Watkins Publishing 2005) p.89
73. Of the contrasting spelling, The *Kabbalah* is the Judaic tradition; *Qabalah* is the mystical version and *Cabbala* the Christian.
74. Howe, p.208
75. A.E. Waite, *Notes on the mysteries of magic as expounded in the occult philosophy of Eliphas Levi* (New York, Kessinger 2005) p.29
76. E. Wallis Budge, *Egyptian Magic* (New York: Dover Publications 1971) pp.4-5
77. Ibid., p.23
78. Regardie, p.207
79. Dion Fortune, *The Training and Work of an Initiate* (London: The Aquarian Press 1955) p.45
80. Regardie p. 125
81. Heraclitus, fragment No. 102
82. Greer Appendix C p.398
83. Gilbert, p.129

84. This system was of great interest to Mathers. He had invented, for his own amusement, 'Enochian Chess', a three dimensional form of the game using small versions of Egyptian gods and goddesses for chess pieces.

85. Crowley was prevented from achieving this grade by the London Temple which, given his later magical pedigree seems rather ironic.

86 R.A. Gilbert, Golden Dawn – Twilight of the Magicians (Wellingborough: The Aquarian Press 1983)

87. Gilbert, p.36

88. Israel Regardie, *The Complete Golden Dawn System of Magic* (Phoenix, Ariz.: Falcon Press 1984)

89. A.E. Waite, *The Mysteries of Magic, a Digest of the Writings of Eliphas Levi* (London: George Redway 1886)

90. Howe, p.89

91. Richardson, p.13

92. R.A. Gilbert, *A.E. Waite, Magician of Many Parts* (Wellingborough: The Aquarian Press 1987) p.361

93. Arthur Ransome, *Bohemia in London* (Oxford: O.U.P 1984) pp.56-94. Greer, p.406

94. Melinda Boyd Parsons, *To All Believers: The Art of Pamela Colman Smith* (Wilmington, Delaware: 1975) p.87

96. Ibid., p.8

97. Stuart R. Kaplan, *The Artwork and Times of Pamela Colman Smith* (New York: U.S. Games Systems Inc. 2009) p. 67

98. Confessions, p.642

99. Greer, p.159

100. Howe, p.181

101. $ 126,000 in today's currency.

102. Howe, p. 206

103. Ibid., p. 239

104. Gilbert, p.80

105. Howe, pp.283-284

106. Crowley, p.177

107. Ibid, p.177
108. Ibid, p.177
109. Howe, p.205
110. Greer, p.250
111. Greer, p.250
112. Letter from Mathers to Yeats in 1901. Howe, p.204.
113. Howe, p.180
114. Crowley, p.225
115. Howe, p.225
116. Israel Regardie, *The Eye in the Triangle – An interpretation of Aleister Crowley* (Las Vegas: Falcon Press 1986) p.27
117. Greer, p.243
118. Howe, p.243
119. Florence Farr, *The Occult Review,* Vol.VIII: No.2 (London: William Rider and Son Ltd. 1908) pp. 87-91.
120. Gilbert, p.69
121. Brandy Williams (ed) *Women's Voices In Magic* (Stafford: Megalithica Books 2009) p. 15-16
122. Howe, p.234
123. George Harper, *Yeats Golden Dawn – The influence of the Golden Dawn on the Life and Art of W.B. Yeats* (Wellingborough: Aquarian Press 1974) p.222
124. Richardson, p.14
125. Gilbert, p.73
126. Greer, p.404
127. http://www.mastermason.com/luxocculta/mcgregor.htm
128. Greer, p.350
129. Howe, p.284
130. Dion Fortune, *Psychic Self-Defense* (Boston: Weiser Books 2001) p.79
131. Ibid., p.88
132. Ibid., p.98
133. Ibid., p.99
134. Richardson, p.27

Bibliography

Apuleius, Lucius, *The Golden Ass – The transformation of Lucius* (London: Penguin 1958)

Boyd Parsons, Melinda, *To All Believers: The Art of Pamela Colman Smith* (Wilmington, Delaware 1975)

Campbell, Joseph, *The Hero with a Thousand Faces* (Princeton: Bollingen 1972) Footnote p.88

Castera, Susan P., *Images of Victorian Womanhood in English Art* (Rutherford N.J.: Farleigh Dickinson University Press 1987)

Colquhoun, Ithell, *The Sword of Wisdom* (New York: G.P. Putnam & Sons 1975)

Crowley, Aleister, *Magic* (London: Routledge & Kegan Paul 1973)

Crowley, Aleister, *Moonchild* (New York: Samuel Weiser 1975)

Farr, Florence, *The Occult Review,* Vol. VIII: No.2 (London: William Rider and Son Ltd. 1908)

Fortune, Dion, *Psychic Self-Defense* (Boston: Weiser Books 2001)

Fortune, Dion, *Through The Gates of Death* (Wellingborough: Aquarian Press, 1968)

Fortune, Dion, *The Training and Work of An Initiate* (London: The Aquarian Press 1955)

Fortune, Dion, *Moon Magic* (New York: Samuel Weiser 1995)

Gilbert, R.A., *A.E. Waite, Magician of many Parts* (Wellingborough: The Aquarian Press 1987)

Gilbert, R.A., *Golden Dawn Companion* (Wellingborough: Aquarian Press 1989)

Gilbert, R.A., *Golden Dawn – Twilight of the Magicians* (Wellingborough: The Aquarian Press 1983)

Gilbert, R.A., *Revelations of the Golden Dawn* (Chippenham: Quantum Publishing 1997)

Greer, Mary K., *Women of the Golden Dawn* (Rochester, Vermont: Park Street Press 1995)

Gurdjieff, G.I., *Flight from Reason* (London: MacDonald 1972)

Gwynn, Stephen (Ed.) *Tributes to the Memory of W.B. Yeats* (London: Macmillan 1940)

Harper, George, *Yeats Golden Dawn – The influence of the Golden Dawn on the Life and Art of W.B. Yeats* (Wellingborough: Aquarian Press 1974)

Hone, Joseph, *W.B.Yeats, 1865-1939* (London: Macmillan 1943)

Howe, Ellic, *Magicians of the Golden Dawn – A Documentary History of a Magical Order* (London: Routledge and Kegan Paul 1972)

Jeffares, A. Norman, *W.B. Yeats – Man and Poet* (London: Routledge & Kegan Paul 1949)

Kaplan, Stuart R., *The Artwork and Times of Pamela Colman Smith* (New York: U.S. Games Systems inc. 2009)

King, Francis, *Ritual Magic in England (1887 to the Present Day)* (London: Neville Spearman 1970)

Knight, Gareth, *Magical Images and the Magical Imagination* (Oceanside, California: Sun Chalice: 1971)

Machen, Arthur, *Things Near and Far* (New York: Alfred A. Knopf 1923)

MacGregor Mathers, S., *The Book of the Sacred Magic of Abra-Melin the Magi* (New York: Dover publications 1975)

MacGregor Mathers, S., *The Key of Solomon the King (Clavicula Salomnis)* (London: Routledge and Kegan Paul 1972)

Maitland, Edward, *Anna Kingsford, Her Life, Letters, Diary and Work* (London: George Redway 1896)

Ozaniec, Naomi, *The Kabbalah Experience – The Practical Guide to Kabbalistic Wisdom* (London: Watkins Publishing 2005)

Pearson, Pearson, *Bernard Shaw – His life and Personality* (London: Methuen 1961)

Ransome, Arthur, *Bohemia in London* (Oxford: O.U.P 1984)

Regardie, Israel, *The Complete Golden Dawn System of Magic* (Phoenix, Ariz.: Falcon Press 1984)

Regardie, Israel, *The Eye in the Triangle – An Interpretation of Aleister Crowley* (Las Vegas: Falcon Press 1986)

Richardson, Alan and Hughes, Geoff, *Ancient Magicks for a New Age* (Minnesota: Llewellyn Publications 1989)

Richardson, Alan, *Priestess – The life and Magic of Dion Fortune* (Wellingborough: Aquarian Press 1987) Wade Allan (ed), *The Letters of W.B. Yeats* (London: Rupert Hart-Davis 1954)

Waite, A.E., Notes on the mysteries of magic as expounded in the occult philosophy of Eliphas Levi (New York, Kessinger 2005)

Waite, A.E, *The Mysteries of Magic, a Digest of the Writings of Eliphas Levi* (London: George Redway 1886)

Wallis-Budge, E., *Egyptian Religion* (New York: Dover Publications 1971)

Wallis Budge, E., *Egyptian Magic* (New York: Dover Publications 1971)

Yeats, W.B., *Stories of Red Hanrahan: The Secret Rose: Rosa Alchemica* (London: Macmillan 1913)

Yeats, W.B., *Autobiographies* (London: Macmillan 1955)

AXIS MUNDI
BOOKS

Axis Mundi Books provide the most revealing and coherent
explorations and investigations of the world of hidden or
forbidden knowledge. Take a fascinating journey into the realm
of Esoteric Mysteries, Magic, Mysticism, Angels, Cosmology,
Alchemy, Gnosticism, Theosophy, Kabbalah, Secret Societies and
Religions, Symbolism, Quantum Theory, Apocalyptic
Mythology, Holy Grail and Alternative Views of Mainstream
Religion.